Forest H. Belt's

Easi-Guide

to

MULTISPEED BICYCLING

Text by

Forest H. Belt and
Bonnie C. Smith

Photography by

Bonnie C. Smith and
Carmen W. Wilson

HOWARD W. SAMS & CO., INC.
THE BOBBS-MERRILL CO., INC.
INDIANAPOLIS · KANSAS CITY · NEW YORK

FIRST EDITION

FIRST PRINTING—1974

Copyright © 1974 by Howard W. Sams & Co. Inc., Indianapolis, Indiana 46268. Printed in the United States of America.

All rights reserved. Reproduction or use, without express permission, of editorial or pictorial content, in any manner, is prohibited. No patent liability is assumed with respect to the use of information contained herein.

International Standard Book Number: 0-672-21096-7
Library of Congress Catalog Card Number: 74-79347

Introduction

The sturdy two-wheel balloon-tire bicycle kids rode just a few years ago has metamorphosed. Today, adults and youngsters alike pedal around on sleek lightweight machines that remind you of racing bikes. Some probably are. But the majority fall into a popular new category: *multispeed bicycles.*

They have gears, like a car. Three-speed, five-speed, and ten-speed models are for "ordinary" riders. Racing cyclists straddle elaborate ten-, fifteen-, and eighteen-speed streamliners. Imported lightweights vie with domestic brands. If you're into bicycling at all nowadays, a multispeed is the only way to go.

Since the multispeed bicycle in such proportions is a new phenomenon, some of its peculiarities are still a mystery to many. Hence this book—put together to help you find the most fun, economy, and dependability a multispeed bike can deliver.

Did you know the bicycle ranks as the world's most efficient transportation? It's true. Measured by the calorie, pedaling consumes less energy per mile traveled than any other kind of transport. That may need some explanation.

Walking takes energy. So does a car—fossil-fuel energy, and lots of it. Riding a horse consumes little of your energy; but the horse expends a lot, which you rebuild with hay and grain. When you toss body weight (or machine-plus-load weight) and speed into an energy-per-mile equation, you come to realize the horse is inefficient. So is a jet airplane. You base these calculations on three things: distance traveled, total weight moved, and calories burned.

A modern bicycle glides along on hard-pressured pneumatic tires. Its geared, ball-bearing smoothness makes effective use of your energy. Pedaling your bicycle a mile takes only one-fifth the calories you would burn walking that far. The reasons are complicated, relating to body position and the distance you move for each leg-muscle contraction. It all boils down to one fact: you and your bicycle represent the most efficient traveling partnership on earth.

Bicycles have come a long way since the first two-wheel velocipede (literally "swift walker") was patented in 1818 by an English coachmaker. It had no pedals; you sat astride and pushed along with your feet on the ground. For the last half-century, the pedal bicycle has supplied transportation for most of the world. In the United States, the automobile overshadowed bicycles; bikes became traditional for children.

And then, in the late 1960s, bicycling in the U.S. abruptly transformed. A penchant for exercise and fresh air drew Americans outdoors, and whole families turned avidly to bicycling. People who count things estimate there are between 80 and 90 million bicycles whisking riders down streets, through parks, and into the countryside. Everywhere you turn, you find cyclists. This book is dedicated to all of them.

Researching and photographing this book, coauthor/photographer Bonnie C. Smith met hundreds of these riders. She went along on tours, pedaled her own bicycle many miles, attended club and association meetings, and visited bicycle dealers and repair shops. The more she immersed herself in bicycling, the more her enthusiasm soared. "That's the way it is with bicycling," she says. Miss Smith had become a photographer-and-writer after a few years of teaching. You can see her photos in other *Forest H. Belt Easi-Guides*.

Carmen W. Wilson, the second photographer for this book, operates his own marketing and advertising services firm. He is staff photographer for a small paper, and specializes in candids and photos for small business. You can see his work too in other *Easi-Guides*.

The three of us thank all the cyclists who contributed in so many ways to this book. For special help we thank the employees and owners of Dayton's Bicycle Co-op, Elson Quality Bikes, and Matthews Bicycle Mart, all of Indianapolis. Mr. and Mrs. Rhodes Dayton and sons Steve and Mark, Wendell Brown, Don Engle, and Mr. and Mrs. Ross Faris pitched in more than we could ever thank them for. Finally we appreciate the information and advice supplied by American Youth Hostels Inc., the Bicycle Institute of America, Chain Bike Corp., Columbia Manufacturing Co., Huffman Manufacturing Co., the National Transportion Safety Board, Original Plastic Bike Inc., Raleigh Industries of America Inc., and Schwinn Bicycle Co. We (and you) owe all these people and companies a special vote of thanks.

Enjoy this book. Its photos and words should help you draw the very best from yourself as a rider and from your multispeed bicycle. I, Miss Smith, and Mr. Wilson wish you many years of happy riding.

Forest H. Belt

Contents

CHAPTER 1

Great New Way to Remain Young 7
    What bicycling is about—Who does it—How they use bicycles—Youngsters — Athletes — Controlling weight and figure — Around town—In the peaceful countryside—Crosscountry—Riding to work

CHAPTER 2

A Bicycle for Every Purpose 21
    The bike you buy depends on what you want it for—On campus—How many speeds—Tandems—Family bikes—Triwheelers—Lightweight bicycles—Special types—Kids' bicycle varieties—Accessories—Unusual bikes

CHAPTER 3

Buying a New or Used Bicycle 35
    What to pay—Where to buy bicycles—Advantages of bike shops—Catalogs—Gear ratios in multispeeds—Welded and lugged frames—Reynolds 531 alloy—Butted tubes—Two kinds of brakes—Multispeed gear shifters—Tires for your riding purposes—How to shop for a used bike—Looking it over thoroughly and trying it out—Making the deal

CHAPTER 4

Riding Multispeed Bicycles 53
    Don't be ashamed to learn—Setting handlebars for the right feel—Saddle height and tilt—Pedals for your kind of riding—The three main kinds of multispeed bikes and their qualities—How to shift gears of a ten-speed machine—Gears of a five-speed—What all the gear ratios are used for and what they do for you—Three-speed is simplest of all

CHAPTER 5

Around Home: Safe City Riding 69
    Traffic laws—Basic turning rules—Left turns in various traffic situations—Right turns are less dangerous—How and when to signal stops—Four-way stop streets—Bad weather and panic stops—Railroad crossings—Which side of the road—Alleyways and pedestrians—Horseplay and stunts—Safety equipment and clothing

CHAPTER 6

Crosscountry Pedaling Trips 81
    Bicycling vacations—Off the beaten track—Touring alone—Bicycle bags to hold supplies—Packing bags—Loading a multispeed bicycle for travel—Clothes to take along—When to stop and rest—Eating along the way—Sleeping accommodations—Keep in touch with home

CHAPTER 7

Some Hints on Bicycle Camping 95
    Combining off-the-highway riding with camping—Where to find campsites—Getting you and your bike to distant camping spots—Camping equipment and food—Preparing yourself for camping

CHAPTER 8

If the Racing Bug Bites 103
    Three kinds of racing—Road racing—Criterium events—Track competition—Qualities of a racing cyclist—The racing bike—Supplies and clothing—Training—Reaching events—Riding techniques winning racers use—Finding out more about races

CHAPTER 9

Maintenance for Safety and Economy 115
    Cleaning and waxing—Repairs for clincher tires—Demounting and remounting the tire—Wheel alignment—Fork troubles—Handlebars and grips—How to tape handlebars—Pedals—Crank care—Cleaning, soaking, and oiling the roller chain—Adjustments for derailleurs—Adjusting the front derailleur—Handbrake care and replacement—Lubrication guide

CHAPTER 10

Clubs and Getting Together 137
    How cycling associations start—What they do and how they go about it—Large and small clubs—Education through club activities—Contests—Neighborhood safety inspection lanes—Organizing hikes and tours—Riding with other clubs and vice versa

Chapter 1

Great New Way to Remain Young

Bicycling has become a happening. Have just one warm day and you see bikes on the streets everywhere. Bike route signs have sprung up around towns all over the country. Families with two and three cars have added a bike for each member.

Bicycle sales are estimated at 12 million a year, and they keep climbing. More than 85 million people use bicycles in an endless variety of ways. The stereotype of bicycling used to be a kid on a bike. Today his mom may ride her bike to the grocery . . . his dad may pedal downtown to his office. Groups take leisurely rides through the countryside.

All ages and types of people are bicycling—some for practical purposes, some for recreation. The gasoline situation spurs a few into buying a bike for transportation. If you haven't yet discovered bicycling, you have some pleasant surprises in store. Turn the next few pages and view some of the enjoyments.

Not many years ago most biking was done by young people. No longer. Now every age group is in on the action.

Many older persons pedal for vital purposes of health. Doctors may recommend exercise to help fight arthritis in legs and hips. One lady rides 5 miles every day, by doctor's orders. Heart attack patients may be advised by their doctor to do light pedaling.

But therapy is not the only benefit. Fresh air and exercise go along with maintaining good health. Bicycling increases circulation and the blood supply to body cells as leg muscles contract and push blood upward. Breathing rate increases, raising the body's oxygen supply. Diaphragm and lungs are strengthened. Better circulation and more oxygen leave almost anyone feeling more energetic and healthy.

If you're an older person whose auto driving is restricted, bicycling gives you a great chance to get out of the house. Minor aches and pains go away as you become more active. Don't sit around and go stale when you retire. And don't blame age for fancied ailments. Bicycle your way to health. It costs less than medicine and doctor bills.

HOWEVER, ASK YOUR DOCTOR'S ADVICE before you do a lot of pedaling. Some illnesses can leave you in a condition that might be jeopardized by exertion.

A bicycle is usually a youngster's first means of independent transportation. Having been only passenger or pedestrian, he gets his first taste of a new viewpoint. He usually becomes a more considerate traveler.

A bike offers a youngster his first big chance to expand socially. He meets more people, and broadens his geographic horizon. A bike provides transportation to club meetings, after-school activities, and local events.

Bikes teach mechanical principles to their young owners. For example, kids can understand better how automobile gears work by relating them to gears on their bikes.

Learning to ride brings emotional growth for small children. They learn the pleasure of attaining a skill, and the reward from not giving up in spite of discouragement. Learning on their own heightens independence.

Owning something like a bike imparts a sense of responsibility, and can help develop it. A bike must be taken care of. He learns to store and lock his bike properly. He may even learn to save money, if he wants accessories. He can learn to be patient until he can afford them.

Older youths find a bike can link them with a job. The newspaper-delivery boy or girl can use a bike to collect as well as deliver. Some kids pedal on errands for the neighbors to earn spending money.

Finally, a bike is one avenue to auto driving skill in the future. The same laws apply to cyclists that apply to drivers. Obeying traffic laws takes on relevance for the young rider.

In neighborhoods occupied by young families, you'll see a lot of bicycle traffic. Spring and summer evenings draw out the bicycles. It's a great way to relieve tensions. During the day, the young wife finds a quick ride around the neighborhood a relaxing change of pace for her child and herself. A child's seat, attached properly, holds a youngster securely. A quick ride for husband or wife (or both) after work is relaxing.

Newly marrieds appreciate how little bicycling costs. Some pedal on Sundays or on days they have off together. A bike trip to a park with a picnic lunch can lengthen into all day outdoors. Bicycling with a club introduces a chance for socializing and for participating in exciting activities.

Bicycling is practical for the budget. You can run errands, or use it as a way to get to work—especially in cities where bike commuter routes have been established.

Each member of your family can have his own bike. You can all share in the pleasure and recreation of biking. Instead of piling into the car, everyone climbs on a bike and the family is off. A large picnic can be divided up so you each tote your fair share.

You'll discover something else when bicycling rather than driving. There's less bickering among the kids. It's hard to be bored pedaling your way somewhere.

Use some imagination to specialize your family's bike activities. If you all enjoy history, cycle to some historic site or to a museum. Your city almost certainly has tourist attractions and places of interest that are feasible for you to ride to. You have to keep distance in mind because of younger family members. Determine how far your family can pedal comfortably before you make too many plans. Start with 5 miles or so, and expand from there. Don't tackle long distances unless everyone has multispeed bikes. Travel no more than half the distance your family can manage; you have to return, you know. Your family may eventually decide to bicycle your whole vacation, touring and camping.

For shorter trips, find bike routes that are marked for cyclists' convenience. Lay out your own favorite way or wander wherever you wish. Taking off with no destination in mind can be as much fun as a planned hike. Try to pass a few places with restrooms and drinking water.

Pedaling with your very young riders to get ice cream or to a baseball game can make a summer evening enjoyable.

Athletes know that pedaling is a great way to stay in shape during the off season. Some coaches insist on bikes as part of the training program.

Cycling can benefit any athlete. Strengthening the diaphragm helps breathing, a special benefit in sports that demand running endurance. Pedaling strengthens leg muscles. Even stomach muscles tone up if you sit properly (leaning forward) as you ride.

If you're an athlete, you can pedal moderately just to keep in shape. If you want to build endurance, concentrate your effort and push yourself to your limit on a bike. You can lose weight if you need to.

Athletes aren't the only ones who can benefit physically from bicycling. Besides keeping weight down, bicycling improves the figure. Waistline and thighs trim down as your muscles become tighter. You can slenderize heavy ankles by pedaling properly (page 57).

One of the nicest things about a bicycle for the figure and weight control: you don't have to join an expensive spa. The bike is convenient and fits anywhere in your schedule. You can even combine exercise with errands you need to run.

Start noticing how slim most people are who cycle regularly. An hour of cycling burns 492 calories. That much every day, if you don't eat more, could trim off 6 pounds a month.

An exercycle is better than nothing. But you miss the scenery. Even more, though, fresh air and improved circulation bring you a clearer complexion. You get sun bicycling, too. Enjoy the neighborhood or countryside. It beats puffing and panting on a hard floor to reduce.

You could ride just for the simple pleasure cycling brings. Biking in the city can be as relaxing as country riding. You may even prefer city surroundings. Shady sidestreets and mildly traveled residential avenues make for enjoyable city riding.

You can discover a whole new facet of your city and neighborhood by bicycling. Being on a bike slows you down enough to appreciate something as ordinary as a well-kept lawn. You might even meet some of your neighbors. New to a neighborhood? Cycling helps you get oriented and learn where things are.

If you want to venture out of the neighborhood, locate some museums, public gardens, parks, zoos, and historic sites. Phone your Chamber of Commerce to find out what your city and nearby towns have to offer. Most civic and cultural events are listed in the newspaper. Pedal to a town festival or fair.

City bike routes generally take you through the more scenic, less traveled parts of the city and suburbs. Bike Route signs keep pointing the direction to take. Bike trails along canals or through parks lend a pseudo-rural effect you might like.

You can enjoy bicycling anywhere. If your city offers none of the things mentioned, seek out your own special places to ride in or near the city.

You may not find that quiet residential area in your part of the city. Being surrounded by busy, heavily used streets doesn't stop the bike enthusiast. He rides wherever is available. Of course, a peaceful ride transforms into an on-guard-for-traffic ride. But with experience you can enjoy yourself. You learn to cope with it by practicing certain safety rules (Chapter 5).

Commuting to work by bike in city traffic isn't all bad. Bicycles often travel faster than cars in rush-hour traffic.

Not all city bike routes meander through sparsely traveled areas. Some forge right down heavily used streets. When you visit downtown points of interest, you're stuck with heavy traffic. Just learn to control your bike well, watch out for thoughtless motorists and pedestrians, and you can ride where you want to.

You find your really peaceful bike riding on trails in the country. They offer a chance to escape city noise and annoyances. You can relax without worrying over traffic or pedestrians.

Nature lover? You can enjoy your bike *and* nature on wooded trails. A good bike is very quiet. You hear only the sound of the wind. You can feel the road's surface. You don't frighten the birds or animals. What surrounds you is the quietness and activity of nature—activity that can only be seen while hiking or biking. You experience the countryside in a new way, more deeply, as you expose yourself to it through bicycling.

A few city parks offer bike trails that have tree and plant overgrowth along the way to give a rural effect. Following established trails lets you be concerned more with your surroundings than with traffic and navigation. You may want to stop, browse, collect trivia, take pictures, or just absorb the quiet. An afternoon on a woodsy trail can send you back home or to work with a refreshed attitude and spirit.

Traveling across the country by bicycle isn't a far-fetched idea. A cyclist who wants to expand his knowledge of people and America finds long-distance cycling a very economical way to do just that. Some riders pedal long distances just to say they've done it. Whatever reason you choose, it's quite an adventure in independence and self-sufficiency.

Not uncommonly, individuals form caravans that take them hundreds of miles together. College groups pedal across the continent every summer. The idea doesn't stop with this continent either; groups travel throughout Europe and tour other foreign countries on their bikes. Youth hostels provide inexpensive lodging; they're also becoming popular in the United States.

Obviously, tour-cycling involves far more than common pleasure riding. Planning is important. So is seriousness about bicycling.

Bicycling is popular because there are so many things you can do—camp, tour, exercise, commute, race. The whole family can take part.

Bicycling as a sport doesn't restrict you to limited areas. Baseball takes a diamond. Boating requires water—a lake or river. Bicycling knows no locale or season. People ride in cold or hot weather, wherever they take a notion.

Some sports—such as rollerskating or swimming—require you to spend money every time you participate. Bicycling is virtually free after you own a bike. A horse needs oats; not your bike. Maintenance cost is low. No special uniforms are required. A bicycle is a lasting investment. The cost of renting ski equipment and spending one day on the slopes would buy a used bike.

Economics keeps recurring as a reason to bicycle. Pedaling to the grocery, for example, is cheaper than driving. Some riders wouldn't have considered a bicycle had the energy crisis not occurred. People ride for recreation. Kids pedal to school. The bicycle is one of the few solutions to gasoline prices. Cyclists breeze right on by those gas pumps.

For some people, the bicycle means only transportation. Nothing wrong with that. It might mean riding a bike in a business suit. It's a healthy, nonpolluting mode of transportion. Environment enthusiasts applaud the benefit to nature. With the gasoline shortage, you know a bike will get you there!

Sometimes it'll get you there faster than in a car. Bike riders whiz right on by backed-up traffic. Indianapolis is one city that has laid out routes that enable cyclist commuters to pedal downtown on safe and fairly direct routes. Some cities have bicycle-only lanes on busy thoroughfare streets. Parking lots that are full of cars can nevertheless hold a few more bikes—and make money from it. Parking your bike is less trouble than parking a car, although you do have to lock your bike properly.

A bike not only gets you there on time, it refreshes you and clears the cobwebs from your mind. You arrive ready for the day. The exercise at the end of the day can unwind you. Just pedal easy and relax your way home.

Sometimes, there's just no figuring out why certain people ride a bicycle. Nor is there any accounting for their taste in machines. Whereas one cyclist goes in for speed and racing sleekness, another may be content to pedal along on the oldest two-wheeler he can lay hands on. The majority, of course, find a pleasant middle ground between great expense and parsimony.

Rest assured about one thing, though. Wherever you encounter a serious bicyclist, chances are high you've found a contented person . . . no matter what he's riding.

Chapter 2

A Bicycle for Every Purpose

No one bicycle fits every need. Your reason for biking dictates the kind of bike you'll want. A lightweight racing bike wouldn't last long for delivering newspapers. The touring cyclist won't go far on a conventional one-speed bike.

At one time, the standard single-speed bicycle was about the only kind used in this country—except for racing. The one-speed is an uncomplicated bike. It has coaster brakes (you operate them by backpedaling). This type of bike is okay if you're a casual cyclist who only rides around the neighborhood once in a while, and are not interested in touring, trips, or cycling over varied road conditions and terrain.

Some people prefer a one-speed for exercising because pedaling is more strenuous. Others like the simplicity—no complicated gears and maintenance. The one-speed bike costs less new or used. It isn't as attractive to thieves. It withstands more abuse. You can find a used one easier.

You can definitely enjoy cycling with a regular bike, and that's the idea behind owning a bicycle anyway.

Life on a large college campus gets hectic. Students walk, run, drive, or pedal across campus to class. Students find bicycles a feasible and wise investment. They're easier to park and cheaper to maintain than cars. A bike takes no money for gasoline.

A bicycle can ease the problem of recreation and entertainment. Many students don't have extra money for movies and eating out. Bicycling dates are enjoyable and cost less than many other activities. Groups and couples can plan bike hikes and outings. Include food, and you have a picnic. You can rent a tandem and take off for a couple hours' relaxation at little cost. Parks near campuses are full of bikes, usually, proving the popularity of college bicycling.

During exams, pent-up weariness from studying can be lightened by a quick bicycle ride. The break refreshes your mind. The exercise benefits your body. Especially where quiet roads or bike trails abound, a slow ride can put you in new spirits.

The question is: what kind of bicycle best suits a college student? The multispeed is most practical for commuting to an off-campus job. It covers longer distances faster and with less wasted energy. Students do own all kinds of bikes—with one, three, five, and ten speeds. For maximum use, the multispeed probably is best. Yet, if you confine your biking to on-campus transport, a one-speed may be more economical.

Kids who fit the age group between high-risers and a ten-speed find the five-speed suitable. You have the advantage of gears. Kids like to go farther afield as they grow older. It's exciting to pedal to a park glade or some other favorite spot to share secrets. That way you make it there in time to enjoy yourself and get home in time for supper.

Five-speeds aren't designed so explicitly for light weight as ten-speeds are. They aren't as much trouble to take care of. Handlebars are usually chrome and upright. You can add drop handlebars. The only gear shift is near the stem. The bike may have fenders front and back, though smaller than on a one-speed. You have rubber pedals, and no toe-clips.

Five-speeds carry you over most hills with ease. For limited traveling, the five-speed serves well.

However, multispeed bicycles have far outstripped the regular bicycle in popularity. Some bike shops today sell nothing but multispeeds. That seems to be where the business is. Experienced cyclists derive much pleasure from riding a multispeed machine.

The ten-speed bicycle is in the most demand. With it, you can choose a gear ratio to suit whatever riding conditions you encounter: uphill, down, flat, fast, slow, and so on.

The three-speed bicycle falls next in popularity. Less complex than a ten-speed, it does make pedaling easier than with a one-speed. The five-speed bike falls between the three- and single-speed. Despite the smaller choice of gears, it has many advantages of the ten-speed.

Skyrocketing interest in touring, racing, and using a bike for transportation is responsible for multispeed bikes being popular. The gears make traveling long distances feasible, because pedaling is not so tiresome. In some localities, varied and rugged terrain demands a bicycle with gears.

Ten-speed machines serve mainly for racing and touring. Three-speed bikes appeal to those who want the advantages of gears without the complications. If you don't feel up to handling ten gears, a three-speed may be a wise compromise. A three-speed is easier to take care of and less susceptible to damage than a ten-speed.

If you pedal frequently around town or ride in hilly places very often, you might pick a five-speed model. You could be as serious about biking as the ten-speed cyclist. But one difference involves distance. A five-speed bike can be used in the same terrain as a ten-speed, but you won't likely use it for long distances. Five-speeds are great for transportation and short-haul bicycling.

Tandem bicycles attract attention. Just seeing one gives many people an urge to try it. Tandems were popular early in this century. With the nostalgia kick so many are on, their popularity has returned.

You can buy three-, five-, and ten-speed tandems. Prices range from $100 to $600. Multispeed tandems make a ride in hilly or steep country less tiring. Many parks with bike-rental shops include one-speed tandems. Sometimes an auto service station near a park rents tandem bikes.

You'll probably like tandems best for recreational riding. They are a little shaky to handle with just one rider, so count on including a partner. A group of couples could organize a tandem race.

Family bicycling is a healthy, inexpensive form of "together" recreation. Multispeed bikes seem to suit this purpose best. Of course, all the members need multispeeds, or lengthy family outings in hilly areas would be nigh impossible. Except to cover less distance when you stay together as a group.

How long should family trips be? Seasoned tourists travel as much as 100 miles in a day; 70 or so would be average. Your family should be able to cover close to 50 miles a day. It's better to underestimate expected distance than to overestimate. Evening rides help condition you for long or short trips.

Springtime, with its freshness, is tops for family bike outings. You see evidences of spring you couldn't from a car. Autumn, too, can be beautiful from a bicycle. Many bicycling clubs have special spring and fall tours in which your entire family can participate.

Some families extend day-long outings to overnight, or even several days. Experienced families camp for weeks by bicycle. Camping, you don't have to handle long distances every day.

Until recently, triwheelers were the orphans of the bicycle world. But today its usefulness makes up for its awkward appearance. Three wheels eliminate the problem of balancing.

You can haul packages care-free. Most triwheelers come with a rear basket already mounted. You can lift it off to carry small packages into the house in one trip. The average basket holds two full grocery sacks, with room left over.

A triwheeler costs from $150 to $250. You can buy a one- or three-speed. Triwheelers are more difficult to store than bicycles because of the width. Consider where you can garage it. Other than that, maintenance cost is very small.

A triwheeler is especially useful and practical for older people. Some are no longer able to balance a two-wheel bike. For the older person without a car or driver's license, a triwheeler puts an end to being stranded at home.

This mode of transportation has other benefits. You can enjoy the out-of-doors on the way to the store. The exercise benefits anyone. (One woman has hers set up indoors in the wintertime, with two boxes under the rear axle. With the wheel turning free, she exercises an hour every morning and afternoon, all winter long.) Pedaling outdoors is easier with gears. In areas with hills and inclines, a three-speed model is almost necessary.

For group riding, you can't beat a ten-speed. Most serious cyclists own a ten-speed because of two main advantages.

One is lightness. When you're pedaling to the park, 10 or 15 extra pounds doesn't interfere. But on a tour of 20 miles or more, those extra pounds are a millstone to you. Because of this, ten-speeds are built from lightweight alloys. Handlebars, cranks, frames, pedals, and rims are designed for lightness. Fenders and heavy chainguards are omitted.

The second advantage is the variety of gears. Ten gear ratios accommodate all kinds of terrain. More important, though, is the "equalizing" effect of ten power ranges. Everyone can adjust the gear they ride in to suit their own leg-strength. The group stays together, even though made up of some strong riders and some weak. They just ride in different gears.

You've been looking at bikes categorized according to speeds or gears. They are also grouped by weight. The one-speed bike falls under the *heavy duty* classification—weighing 40 lb or more. It doesn't need to be lightweight. It can be bounced around and ridden roughly with no harm done. A three-speed weighs about the same as a one-speed, and is almost as sturdy.

Five- and ten-speed bikes are *lightweights.* Ten-speeds weigh from 16 to 39 lb. Five-speeds, from 20 to 35 lb. A lighter bike responds more quickly to the rider. Racing bikes are extremely lightweight because of this need for responsiveness. Attaining and maintaining speed depend upon the weight of the bike. Even a couple of ounces can determine a winner. A heavier bike adds road and wind friction. The racer doesn't need that.

You want lightness for traveling. A few pounds of extra weight can be felt when you pedal several hours. Don't add accessories unless you absolutely need them.

Type of material used for the frame influences weight. Aluminum and its alloys are preferred over steel. Alloy cranksets weigh less than their steel counterparts. Rims and tires make a difference; narrow tire sizes lighten a bike.

Lightness has some disadvantages. You must avoid careless riding. Lightweight rims get bent with mistreatment. Sew-up tires (very lightweight) are temperamental; you can't travel on all road surfaces with them. For this reason, most riders compromise on lightness. They may use clincher tires rather than sew-ups. Others may settle for a slightly heavier frame, too.

Any bicycle can be made lighter. Merely remove paraphernalia. Look at a racer ten-speed. You won't see long metal chainguards, fenders, speedometers, odometers, lights, etc. These cause a bike to drag. They aren't necessary to operation. Remove all this excess trim from your bike—even if it's a one-speed—and you will ride farther, faster, and easier.

Some bicycles adapt to unique situations. Victims of crippling diseases need special kinds of bikes. This brings them the freedom others have. In some cases, the bicycle has therapeutic value of its own, besides that offered by the independence of transportation.

The rider in this photo has been handicapped his entire life. Walking is difficult but he can pedal satisfactorily. His tri-wheeler needs no balancing. Real fresh-air exercise might be otherwise impossible. The three-wheel bicycle broadens this man's horizons immeasurably.

Kids are impressed with high-rise handlebars, banana seats, small wheels, bright colors, and sporty names. The high-risers are distinctive. Some have slicks (tires with no tread). Front wheels are often smaller than rear wheels, to give a "chopped" appearance.

You can buy one-, three-, or five-speed high-risers. Gear shifts on the top tube resemble the "four-in-the-floor" of Dad's car. Beware of the danger in short gear-changer handles; they can injure a child if he falls. Three- and five-speed high-risers have handbrakes instead of coaster brakes.

Another appealing aspect is the countless accessories available to "customize" the bike. Turn signals, mirrors, and chrome parts turn a bike into a juvenile's "car." Teens have sports cars and chopper cycles; preteens have their high-risers.

Some kids handle multispeed bicycles with no problem. A three-speed makes a good beginner's bike. They learn young to handle gear-shifting.

Bikes for youngsters are listed according to wheel size. Frame size has to be considered too. Don't make the mistake of buying a bike your child can "grow into." This can be dangerous. He may not be able to steer or handle it correctly. It might also discourage him since it will make riding more difficult. When he outgrows his bike, sell it used or hand it down to the next member of the family.

Bicycle accessories abound. Walk into most bike shops and you'll see a wall full of useful or ornamental stuff. Prices range from cheap to expensive.

A bike trailer can make owning a bicycle more practical. You can include very tiny children in family rides. In chilly weather, it's easy to wrap a blanket around little ones to keep them warm. This wouldn't be as easy with a child's seat.

Wide selections of bags attach to front bars, behind the seat, or on either side of the back. Carriers and hod panniers keep cycling bags from rubbing against tires. Touring cyclists aren't the only ones who can use bags. Take along a snack, a camera, a notebook, a book to read.

You can buy bicycle radios that mount on handlebars. Look at streamers and wheel decorations. Safety reflectors and reflective tape let you be seen easier at night. Mirrors, horns, lights, automatic rear turn signals, and safety flags are all items that are also decorative.

Serious cyclists buy things like clips for pants, water tanks, tool kits, auxiliary tire pumps, and dog repellent. Some shops carry whole cycling outfits: gloves, racing helmets, and shoes.

Browse around a bike shop. When you buy them thoughtfully, accessories can improve your biking pleasure immensely.

Unusual bicycles include the folding type. It's jointed in the middle. You pull a pin, and the bike stores more compactly. You can keep it in a closet. If you ride to work, a folding bike can be collapsed and set in a corner indoors.

Folding bicycles are also easy to take along on vacation. They fit neatly into a car trunk or the baggage compartment of a light plane. You can incorporate a little pedaling for extra recreation. If your car runs out of gas, you could even pedal to a station!

An even newer phenomenon is the plastic bicycle. The frame, cogs, chain—virtually all parts are made of plastic. They are less expensive to replace than metal parts, and they can't corrode or rust.

A plastic bike is extremely lightweight, under 20 lb. They are not yet in wide supply. Before you buy one make sure parts are available for it.

There are some weird bicycles around. Some aren't even bicycles—the *unicycle* for example. Its appeal lies in its novelty. Anything different usually finds followers. Riding a unicycle looks easier than it actually is. But it's interesting to try, at least.

Some youngsters turn their own bikes into novelty machines by changes which they make on their own. Changing types or sizes of wheels makes a "chopper" or "drag" bike that no manufacturer ever produced. Weird handlebars and seats add to the image. Building a bike from a variety of odd parts creates some strange objects that vaguely resemble bicycles.

But, what the heck . . . these bikes attract attention. They are mainly for creative expression anyway. They may not be as practical as the original, but they're just as much fun—or more —for their owners.

Chapter 3

Buying a New or Used Bicycle

If you're in the market for a new or better bike, you'll want to take several factors into consideration. Spending $100 or more for a bike deserves some thought. Before you even start shopping around, sit down and answer a question or two.

How will you use your bicycle? A $400 machine for errands would be ridiculous. Think about both now and the future. For example, touring may not be in your immediate plans, but does it interest you? You want to buy a bicycle that suits both present needs and whatever other biking activity might attract you. You can lose money trading your bikes too soon or too often.

With a better idea of what you're looking for, your bicycle shopping is ever so much easier.

Give a lot of thought to where you buy your bike. A discount or department store can usually save you money—at least initially.

But remember that you may have to take a fancy bicycle to a bike shop for assembly and adjustment. That'll cost you between $10 and $20. Assembling a bike may sound easy. But when all those nuts, bolts, and screws of a multispeed machine are scattered in front of you, and you have only a skimpy owner's manual to instruct you, your feelings could change.

It's good to try out the bicycle you intend to buy. A particular ten-speed may not be what you imagined. Few department stores can let you try out a bike. But they should be able to help you pick the right frame size and see that your bike has proper seat and handlebar adjustment. Unfortunately, too often the salesperson at a department store has only a vague interest in bicycles, and is not very well informed. He may not be able to answer your questions correctly or help in selecting the right bike. In that event, find another store.

A department or discount store's responsibility usually ends when you carry out the box containing your bike. Check to see that every part is in the box as soon as you get it home. Then, after you have it put together, try to find a bike shop that will adjust the chain and brakes, align the wheels, inflate the tires to correct pressure, and tighten loose nuts and bolts.

Buying from a bicycle shop offers advantages. The dealer often has been in the business most of his life. His only business, very likely, is selling and repairing bicycles. He can give you sound advice and answer all your questions about bicycles. This helps you choose the model best suited to your needs.

Some bike shops specialize. They lean toward certain types of machines, such as ten-speeds only, or maybe foreign makes. So check bike-shop ads in the Yellow Pages. Visit several places you've picked, to compare prices. Ask around. Friends can recommend dealers they have been satisfied with.

Dealers back up the guarantees on their merchandise. If something goes wrong, you'll find it easier to get satisfaction about it. A bicycle shop generally has personnel trained to handle bike problems. Some conscientious dealers offer a free checkup 30 days after you buy a new bike, to make any necessary adjustments.

Consider future repairs. Department stores don't repair bikes. Shops almost always have technicians familiar with the type of bikes they sell.

Many dealers offer items to customize your bike. They can alter features you don't like. Friendliness and helpfulness are a bonus. Usually a dealer can help you locate bicycling clubs. Shops also may stock maps of bicycle routes and pamphlets that help you learn to ride safely.

A majority of serious cyclists feel buying from a catalog is the least satisfactory way to acquire a bicycle. You can't always be sure of the quality some stores offer. Off-brand parts are hard to get, which makes a bike hard to repair. Repair shops seldom carry parts for catalog brands, so repairs are further complicated.

You don't get to try out a catalog bicycle or check whether the frame size fits you. Most catalogs contain a chart which helps determine size, but the surest way is still the straddle method. The long-time, reputable catalog companies guarantee the bicycle against defects, but they can't assure fit.

You assemble your own catalog bike or have a shop do it for you. And someone has to make all those adjustments: handlebars, seat, brakes, and derailleur. An amateur can mess things up.

Don't forget to add freight when you compare catalog prices with the deal you're offered at a bicycle shop.

You'll be concerned with gear ratios when you shop for a multispeed bicycle. At left above, you see a *cogwheel* (*cog* for short), with teeth around its perimeter. A roller chain passes around this cog. The cogwheel attaches solidly to the hub of the bicycle's rear wheel. The chain drives the cog, which turns the rear wheel.

A *sprocket,* up forward on the bicycle, also has teeth over which the chain passes. A *crank* with pedals lets your feet turn the sprocket wheel. That's what drives the chain, which applies motive power to the rear wheel through the cog.

Five- and ten-speed bicycles have five cogs in one assembly at the rear hub. Each cog is a different diameter, with a different number of teeth. Up front, a five-speed bike has a single sprocket (sometimes called *chainwheel*). A ten-speed machine has a double sprocket attached to the crank, with a large wheel and a smaller one. The chain can be on either front sprocket and on any rear cog, depending on where you set the gear-change levers.

The object of gears is to adjust your pedaling power. They're like gears in an automobile. The "highest" gear on a ten-speed machine, for example, places the roller chain around the smaller of the two sprocket wheels and the largest of the five rear-hub cogs. Each pedal revolution (by your feet) results in the farthest possible distance traveled by the rear wheel. Speed is therefore greatest, but pedal pressure required also is heaviest.

The "lowest" gear, on the other hand, places the chain on the larger front sprocket and on the smallest of the five rear cogs. One revolution of the pedal crank doesn't turn the rear wheel very far, but your pedal pressure exerts tremendous power.

Looked at another way, high gears let your pedaling feet turn the crank more slowly for higher over-the ground speeds, but you don't have much power for upgrades or headwinds. Low gears make your feet pedal faster, with slower over-the-ground speed, but you have the power you need to climb steep hills.

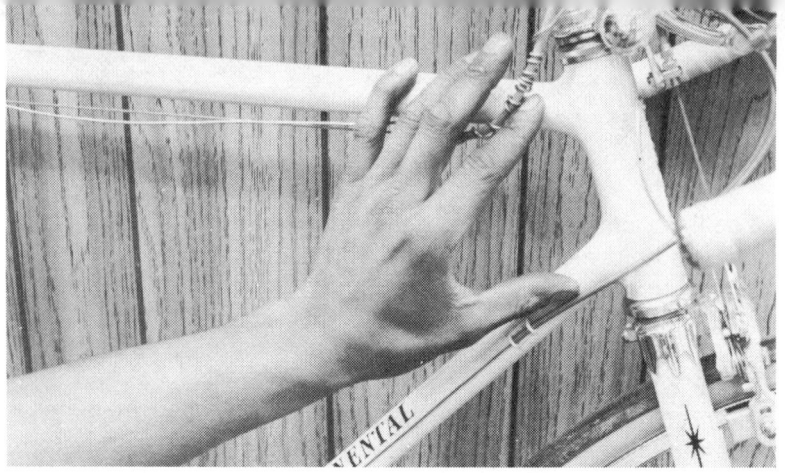

To buy wisely, look at certain things about the construction of a bicycle you like. There are two main ways the frame tubes are joined—welded and lugged.

The steel tubes of a *welded* frame (above) are joined (obviously) by welding. Steel is heavier than other bicycle alloys, so you'll find that most heavier bikes are welded. Welded frames are appropriate for the average adult cyclist, for rough riding, and for young bike owners. Welds are deemed stronger for steel than lugged joints.

The tubes in a *lugged* frame are put together by separate fittings called lugs. Notice where the tubes join (photo below). The lugs are extra lips of metal the tubes fit into.

For lightweight alloys, a lugged frame is considered stronger than a welded one. Lugging lightens the bicycle, giving it a more responsive feel. Most serious cyclists thus prefer the lugged frame. But it depends on how you plan to use your bike. You can get the lugged frame on bikes costing $100 and up, but it costs more than an equivalent model with welded frame. If bicycle weight is important to you, buy a lugged frame.

There's a special type of aluminum alloy called *Reynolds 531*. It is considered superior for frame-tube construction in bicycles.

Many expensive lightweight bikes use Reynolds 531 aluminum. You'll spot a decal, on the tube below the seat, that lists what parts are formed from the Reynolds 531 alloy. If the Reynolds 531 designation is printed slantwise on the decal, it means *all* the frame, including the fork, is made of this special metal.

The strength of Reynolds 531 makes possible a special construction known as *butted tubes.* These tubes make the bike frame even lighter than regular 531 tubes. Instead of having a consistent thickness the entire length of the tube, the wall of a butted tube is thin near the middle and thickens near the ends. That's where the lugging is, and where more strength is needed. Your eye can't distinguish this. The 531 decal stipulates if butted tubing is used.

Reynolds 531 might not be worth the added expense to you. But it is if you put top priority on lightness. Bikes built with Reynolds 531 aren't made for harsh treatment. The frame is strong and responsive, but this kind of bike must be ridden and maintained properly.

Conventional one-speed bikes come with coaster brakes. You backpedal the crank to apply them. The brake mechanism is inside the rear hub.

Multispeed bikes "freewheel," but they shouldn't be backpedaled. They have handbrakes, operated by squeezing brake levers near the handlebar grips. There are two levers—the right one for the rear-wheel brake and the left one for front wheels. You must always squeeze the right (rear) handbrake first, or apply the most pressure there if you need front and rear braking at the same time. You'll go tumbling over the handlebars if you apply only the front brake, particularly if you have to turn simultaneously.

Handbrakes cause special shoes to rub against the wheels' rims. Friction slows the wheel to a stop. The shoes fit on a pair of pivoted arms, called *calipers.* One goes on each side of the wheel rim. A cable runs from the hand lever to the caliper. You squeeze the lever, and the caliper arms pivot and press the brake shoes in against the rims.

Brake styles vary. You find two mainly: one that pulls from the center above the two caliper arms and one that pulls on the arms from one side. Thus you have *side-pull* and *center-pull* caliper brakes.

Cyclists argue back and forth over which is better. Some say the feel of the side-pull isn't definite enough. Others say sidepulls stop the bicycle best. A lot depends on how they feel to you. Some brands give you a choice between the two on certain models.

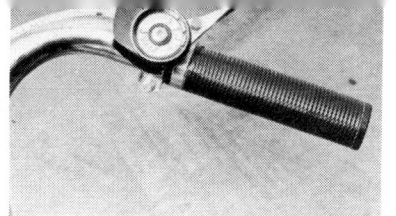 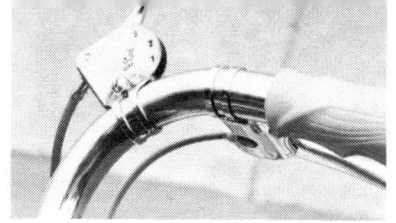

You shift gears on multispeed bicycles with two levers (ten-speed) or one (five- and three-speed). Shifters are located in one of three positions.

A three-speed shifter pod usually mounts on the handlebar, near the right grip. It connects by cable to a mechanism inside the rear hub, which transfers rear-cog turning energy to the bicycle wheel directly or through internal gear arrangements.

A five-speed shifter—one lever—can be on the front tube or on the handlebar stem. Its cable connects to a derailleur mechanism that flips the roller chain from cog to cog at the rear hub.

A ten-speed shifter has two levers, on the stem or on the top tube. The right lever operates the rear-cog derailleur the same as for five speeds. The left lever manipulates a chain-diversion assembly at the double sprocket of the crank, moving the chain to one or the other of the two sprocket wheels.

Whatever the mechanism, shifting should be smooth and quick. The lever should be where you can handle it best.

Part of buying a bike involves selecting tires. You specify rims for the type and size of tire you want. There are two major types of tires for multispeed bikes—clinchers and sew-ups. These are then separated according to size. The main difference between clinchers and sew-ups lies in the way the tire is made.

Sew-up tires contain rubber inner tubes which hold the air. The tubes are totally surrounded by the rubber tire, which is sewn together in the center where it fits against the bicycle rim. Glue or a special tape holds the sew-up tire to the rim. If a sew-up is mounted correctly, it adheres more tightly to the rim the more you ride on it. But it can come off while you're riding if you didn't put it on properly.

Many expensive lightweight bikes come with sew-ups. Because of the thin layers of rubber that keep them light, they puncture easily. They can't take rough treatment and they're harder to repair than clinchers. Some shops won't mess with them.

Sew-ups were created originally for racers. Today, some touring cyclists prefer them over clinchers. Air pressure in them may be as high as 125 pounds per square inch (psi). This gives them low road friction, and they respond to the rider quickly.

And you can prolong the life of a sew-up. Learn to avoid nails and glass. If you can't miss chuckholes and ruts, lift yourself off the seat so your legs will absorb the shock. Walk your bike across railroad tracks or ties. Deflating the tires when you're not riding prolongs sew-up life.

Bikes with sew-ups cost as much as $100 more than the same bike with clinchers. Be sure sew-ups are what you want.

 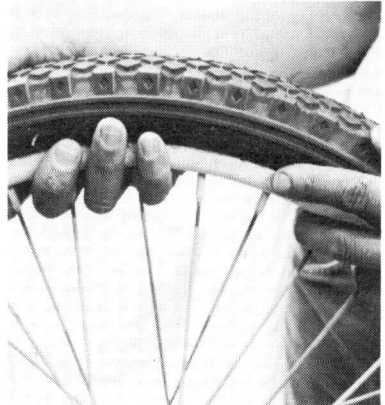

Clinchers are a heavy-duty tire compared to sew-ups. They also have an inner tube. But the tube is not completely surrounded by the tire as with a sew-up. Clinchers contain a metal wire inside the edge (bead) of the tire. It fits inside the edge of the wheel rim. When you pump air into a clincher, the metal-wire edge grips the rim and holds the tire and tube in place. No glue is needed.

Repairs to clinchers are simple. With an inexpensive repair kit, you can repair the tire yourself (pages 118–120). Clinchers are less likely to go flat anyway. Thick layers of rubber make them more durable. But that also increases weight, which decreases their popularity some.

Sew-ups are used only on ten-speed machines. Standard wheel diameter is 27 inches. Sew-up width is 1⅛ inch. The designation used is 27 × 1⅛.

Clinchers come in a variety of wheel diameters and widths. You buy them accordingly. Widths include 1¾, 1⅜, and 1¼. A common clincher tire for a ten-speed bike is designated 27 × 1¼. Clinchers of the 1¼ size are also called touring tires. The less tire that touches the road surface, the less rolling resistance you feel in pedaling. Wide clinchers are best for bikes with heavy frames, such as a one-speed bike or many three-speed models.

Newspaper want-ads are one place to look for a used bike. Try all the local newspapers, even the small "shopper" kind. And look for several weeks, not just once. Circle ads which interest you.

Be alert when dealing with people you don't know. Set up a time when you can check the bike over and test-ride it. If the owner objects to this test ride, forget that bike.

When you buy a reconditioned bike from a shop, there's usually some sort of guarantee to partially protect you. When you buy from an individual, you're on your own. Go over all the things on the following pages. Or, take it to a bicycle shop for checking. The charge is usually small. The owner may not agree. He may not want to risk parting with his bike (he doesn't know you either) nor take the time to go with it to your bicycle technician.

Buying a used bike has disadvantages. You may not be able to find exactly what you want. Don't settle for one you don't want, merely to save money. Shop around some more. Don't give up too soon on finding a used bike you'd like.

It's only fair to consider whether the intended rider likes the bike. With younger ones, observe their initial reaction. First reactions usually display how they truly feel—although that can change. Try to have an idea of what you or the rider wants before you dash out and buy the first used bike you come across. Don't waste money on something that will sit in the garage.

Have the rider try the bike out. Make sure the frame size fits. Be sure, on multispeed bikes, that the gears change correctly and smoothly; they should not make noise when they derail.

Squat down in front of the bike. Look along the head tube and seat tube. Are they aligned? If they're even slightly off, the bike may have been in an accident. The frame could be warped or otherwise damaged. A bent or cracked frame or fork can be expensive to get fixed. Either can be replaced, but that isn't usually worth the expenditure on a used bike. Straightening a frame, which weakens it anyway, costs from $10 to $30, if you can find a shop equipped to do it.

A crooked, bent, or cracked frame is dangerous. Steering is difficult. Bypass a bike with frame troubles.

Turn the bike over so it rests on the handlebars and seat. First, look at the tires. Are the sidewalls scuffed, or do they show other signs of rough treatment? Is the rubber cracked? How worn is the tread? New tires will cost you from $7 on up.

Look for uneven tire wear. The wheels may need realignment, at a cost of from $5 to $15, depending on how many spokes needed replacing.

Check each spoke by plucking it. It shouldn't feel loose. If any of the spokes are too tight or loose, the tire rim probably is crooked. This directly affects tire wear. Spokes which are broken can be replaced for under $1 each. If the spokes have been loose for quite some time, the bike might need a new rim.

Spin the wheels by hand. Listen for any strange sounds. A grinding noise points to faulty bearings. A hub overhaul costs from $5 to $10. Be sure the tires don't rub against the fenders. You may be able to straighten an obstructing fender yourself, without tools, or it may need reshaping.

While the bike is still upside down, look under the fenders for rust which might be hidden when the bike is upright. Also look at the chain and sprocket as you turn them by hand. Is either one rusty or too oily? You can replace the roller chain for about $3, so that's no reason to turn down the bike. On a multispeed bike, an overly oily chain may have brought on a gritty, dirty, malfunctioning derailleur.

Turn the bike several ways, so you can check for rust or damage in all the joints. If rust is only minor, new paint cures that.

Go over the bike for missing parts. If the bike doesn't have fenders and you want them, you'll have to buy them. Check small things closely. Be sure pedals spin freely, and aren't worn thin. Make sure the front light works. A new battery may not solve the problem, especially if the housing looks corroded. If there are no reflectors on the back, you'll have to buy some.

Check handlebars. Look for corrosion spots on chrome finish. Do the handlebars need retaping? Will you need new grips? Look at the seat; it may be too worn for comfort.

Finally, take hold of the bike at the head tube and handlebars and give it a heavy shake. It should not rattle or feel loose. Some nuts and bolts may need to be tightened. However, if they have been loose a long while, other problems may soon develop because of unwarranted wear.

If you can't save money buying a used bike, buy a new one instead. To figure it out, put down how much the owner wants for the used bike. Add the cost of missing parts or needed repairs. Consider the reduced life expectancy of a used bike. Price a comparable new bike. The used one may end up more expensive.

If you write a check, it serves as a receipt. If the seller won't accept a check from a stranger, make sure you get a written receipt. That's your only proof of purchase. You might want proof of ownership, if you have doubts.

You may want to take your used bike to a shop anyway, for a general maintenance checkup. It'll cost several dollars, but you'd be assured the bike is safe. Or, buy your used bike from a reputable dealer. However, check it just as thoroughly as if you were buying it from a private owner.

Chapter 4

Riding Multispeed Bicycles

If you've never ridden a multispeed bicycle, you have a little learning to do, even if you can ride a one-speed. If you don't ride at all, you'd best learn to ride on a regular coaster-type bike before you tangle with a multispeed. The one-speed bike doesn't have extra gadgets like gear and brake levers to confuse you. A beginner needs to concentrate on balancing and steering rather than on what gear to use and when and how.

A regular bicycle usually is thought of as being for the age group below 12. Don't let that stereotype deter you from learning on a regular bike. You'll be a better rider when you finally move to a geared bicycle. Also, a one-speed is more difficult to damage. Letting a multispeed clatter on the ground can damage costly gear-change mechanisms. A delicate bike can be ruined riding it if you don't know what you're doing.

There are certain principles to understand if you want the most enjoyment from riding a multispeed. This chapter explains some of them.

Three- and five-speed bicycles come with upright handlebars. You can change them to *drop* handlebars, the type ten-speed bikes have. Whichever you prefer, you should be able to grip handlebars firmly from your normal riding position. If you can't reach the handlebars easily, you must do one (or all) of three things: (1) adjust the seat; (2) adjust the handlebar; (3) get a frame that fits you. If your knees bump the handlebars, you have too small a frame. With the right frame size, you can straddle the bike comfortably with the top tube almost against your crotch. If you can lift the frame toward you more than an inch, you need a larger frame. If you can't straddle the frame, it's too large for you. Riding will be difficult in either case.

Now, about the handlebars. There are two adjustments. A binder bolt at the top of the handlebar stem lets you set the height of the crossbar. It should be no higher than the saddle or seat. It can be slightly lower, depending on the shape of the handlebars and the position in which you ride. Also align the bar straight across, *exactly* perpendicular to the frame's long axis. If the handlebars become slightly diagonal, your steering judgment may be hampered.

The second adjustment is the head clamp that lets you rotate the crossbar to put the grips up or down where you want them. Upright handlebars put you in a different riding position than do drop types. The facing page discusses how you should be positioned. Read it before you make this final handlebar adjustment.

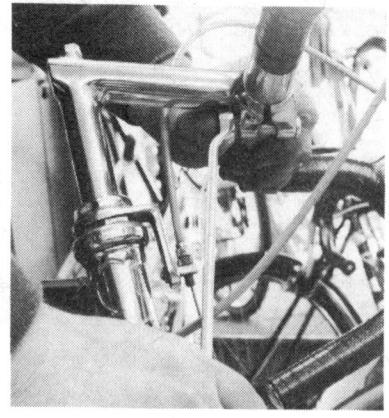

Upright handlebars should be adjusted to a comfortable position that lets you lean slightly forward. Where you hold the grips influences whether you sit straight or lean forward. Many people use upright handlebars because they don't want to lean forward, but they don't usually take long rides.

If you've never ridden a ten-speed, the rider's position may look uncomfortable or unsafe. It's not. With properly set drop handlebars, you're forced to lean down and bend forward. This position lessens tension on any one muscle and it distributes your weight evenly on the bike. You can better utilize your energy in this position. Wind resistance is less, and that makes riding easier. This position also puts you in a natural rolling position if you should happen to fall.

The first few rides may not convince you, but the more and farther you ride, the better you'll appreciate this position. You'll eventually prefer it over sitting straight.

Hand position influences the angle at which you lean forward. Riders put their hands in just about every position on the handlebars. For best steering and safest riding, your hands should be in the curve (corner) near the brake levers. If that's uncomfortable, the handlebars or the saddle may be adjusted wrong. The best position is the one that's most comfortable, provided you can manipulate the brake levers. (Some brakes have a double lever so you can reach them from drop or corner position.)

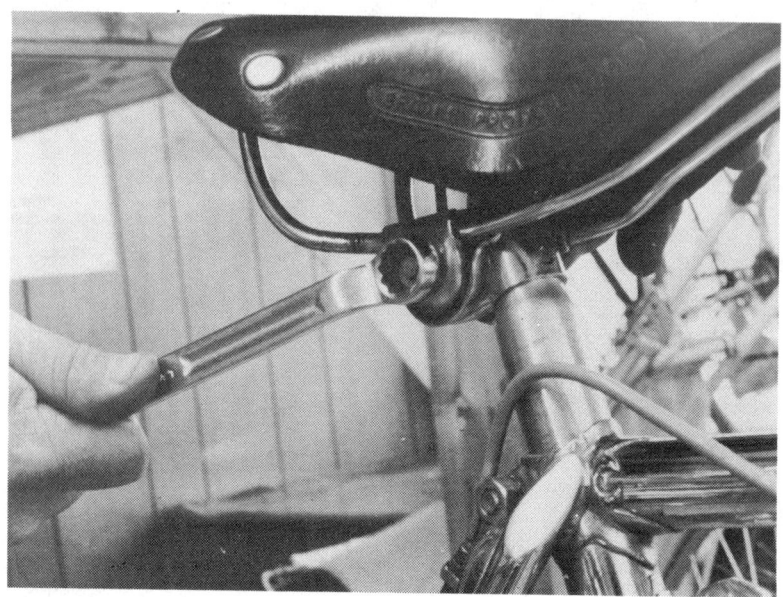

Along with proper frame size and correct handlebar adjustment, saddle height and tilt are factors that enable you to ride your bike comfortably in the correct position. Don't be slavish to rules. You may have the bike adjusted right technically, but still not be comfortable. Start from what's specified, and then alter a little at a time to find what suits you best.

If the saddle is not in the right place, you can't pedal correctly. To test the saddle, sit on it. Your heel (in sneakers or barefoot) should just reach the pedal in the lowest position. If you can bend your knee, the saddle needs to be raised. If your heel doesn't touch the pedal, lower the saddle.

To adjust the seat, first loosen the bolt that locks the saddle stem tightly in the frame tube. That's the bolt down below the wrench in the photo. Loosen the bolt enough that the stem raises and lowers easily. Position the saddle where it should be and tighten the bolt. Recheck from your sitting position on the seat.

Most long-distance riders like the seat tilted backward slightly. The angle for you depends on what's comfortable. Try several and decide which one gives the best ride. To make the adjustment, loosen the clamp nut immediately under the seat (the wrench in the photo). Set the tilt. Don't forget to tighten the nut securely; a loose saddle can be dangerous.

 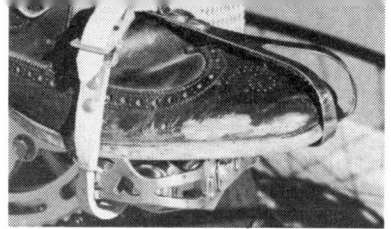

There are two main pedal types—rat-traps and rubber. If you do much riding, your ten-speed will probably already have rat-trap pedals. Rubber pedals come on regular bikes and on most three- and five-speed bikes. Rat-traps are all-metal, with no rubber pads. They are much lighter than rubber pedals, too.

You can add rat-trap pedals to any bicycle. They help your shoe-sole grip the pedal to prevent your foot sliding off.

Toe-clips attach to rat-trap pedals and help even more to keep your foot in place. They are an excellent aid to proper pedaling. Get a set of toe-clips if you plan to do much bicycling. They take some getting used to. The main problem is getting the second foot in when you start off. Practice takes care of that.

Many cyclists don't pedal like they should. Correct pedaling uses leg muscles efficiently. The usual mistake comes when you've pushed the pedal to its lowest point and start returning it to the highest point. The inexperienced rider does nothing as the pedal swings backward—just lets it go till it's at the top and ready for another push downward. This wastes energy. It makes the opposite leg have to push harder.

The solution: Keep the ball of your foot on the pedal. As the pedal is going through that lowest point, continue the pressure, pushing backward and upward. This follow-through in your pedaling is called *ankling.* It can save you 10 to 20 percent in effort on each crank turn.

For general use, there are only three varieties of multi-speed bicycle: three-, five-, and ten-speed. Actually, this means each has that number of gear ratios to choose from. A few special racing machines have 15 or 18 different gear ratios.

The three-speed machine looks different and operates differently than the five- and ten-speed kind. Gear changes are made inside the rear hub. Let your eye follow the cable from the gear-shift lever on the handlebar to the rear wheel. It leads to a switch-like device sticking out the end of the hub.

The gears on three speeds are less complicated, making them easier for some people to operate. A three-speed bicycle doesn't have a very wide range of gear ratios, but those it does have make pedaling more adaptable than with a one-speed bike. The gear lever is marked to indicate each gear. You just flip a lever or slider to whatever gear suits your pedaling at the moment. (You'll see how to decide when to shift, later in this chapter.)

Five- and ten-speed bikes change gears at the rear hub through use of a device called a *derailleur.* You should understand its operation. When you move a lever up front, this device derails the chain from one cog and throws it onto another. This can happen only as you're pedaling. That is, the derailleur pulls the chain sideways and lifts (or drops) it onto the cog adjacent to the one it's on. But, as shown by the front sprocket pair in the photo below, only as the cog or sprocket continues to turn can the chain "follow" onto the newly chosen gear cog. Thus, you cannot shift gears except when pedaling.

Ten-speed bikes have two derailleurs—one at the rear hub and one at the crank. The front one derails the chain onto the second sprocket. This crank or front derailleur is far less elaborate than the one at the rear hub. It guides the roller chain back and forth between only two diameters. The hub derailleur must deal with five different diameters. At the rear, a spring-loaded idler (extending downward from the derailleur) takes up slack in the lower (return) reach of the chain.

Gear-shift levers are located on the straddle tube or on the handlebar stem of ten- and five-speed bikes. Cables connect the gear levers to the derailleurs.

The derailleur on a five-speed bicycle usually looks the same as that used for ten speeds. The difference between the drives of the two bicycles lies at the crank, which has no derailleur and only one sprocket. The rear hub contains a five-gear cog assembly. That's what gives the five gear ratios or speed ranges.

A five-speed bike usually has a 46-tooth sprocket at the crank, and a cog assembly with 14, 17, 21, 26, and 32 teeth. This covers the most useful gears, but the steps between them are greater than if the crank had a double sprocket as it does on a ten-speed machine.

The five-speed bike ordinarily has a heavier frame than the ten-speed (opposite page). There's only one shift lever on the front tube or the stem of a five-speed bike, since there's only one derailleur to be controlled. Pages 66 and 67 explain more of how the tooth ratios on the sprocket and cogs affect pedaling power and bicycle speed.

Ten-speed bicycles are the Cadillacs of bicycling. They offer the widest range of gears and so give more freedom from pedaling fatigue. You can conquer all kinds of terrain with a ten-speed.

At the rear wheel hub, you see the five toothed wheels that make up the rear cog assembly. Each wheel, being a different diameter, determines how far the rear wheel turns each time the pedal crank revolves. The ratios of their diameters to the crank-wheel diameters determine the pedal pressure you have to exert to ride up or down various grades.

Look at the front. The ten-speed has a double sprocket. The five-speed has one. Two (sprockets in front) times five (cogs in back) equals ten (speeds or gear ratios). A racing bike with three crank sprockets gives you fifteen speeds or gears.

Count the number of teeth on each rear cog, starting with the largest (closest to the spokes). The largest cog, with the most teeth, forms half the lowest gear. The smaller of the crank sprockets is the other half. Low gear makes pedaling effort easiest. You exert the least leg force to move you and the bicycle forward. You pay for this effort economy by going the least distance for each crank turn. The rear wheel does not travel as many feet per pedal revolution in low gear as it does in higher gears. The next four pages explain the details of these gear ratios and how you can use them.

Experience more than anything else will teach you which gear to use. Since five- and ten-speed bikes don't have marked levers, you learn to "feel" the right gear.

The basic idea behind when to shift is simple. When your feet spin the pedals rapidly and you seem to be getting nowhere, shift to a higher gear. If pedaling feels hard, shift down. You'll quickly acquire a feel for gears and picking the right one for your riding style will become automatic.

There's another factor to consider in choosing the gear for a particular pedaling condition. You pedal most efficiently when you're turning the crank between 60 and 80 revolutions per minute. That's about one full turn per second. If you choose a gear that lets you pedal at that rate, at the same time letting you apply a pedal pressure that is standard for you, you'll travel almost tirelessly.

For most riding, you only need to shift one lever at a time. The back-and-forth juggling between gear levers could become a nuisance and confusing if you try to go through each gear in sequence, as with a car. You don't have to. You can leave the left lever forward or up, which keeps the chain on the smaller front sprocket. On some bikes, that gives you gear one, three, five, seven, or nine, depending on which rear cog you select with the right lever. On others, you get gear one, two, four, six, or eight (page 64). That's plenty of ranges for ordinary riding. You could have gear two, four, six, eight, or ten by leaving the left lever toward you (down)—or three, five, seven, nine, or ten, again depending on the bike. The large front sprocket holds the chain.

The levers on some brands operate the opposite. The bike used for illustration on these pages works as described. You have what are considered three low gears, four general-purpose gears, and three high gears. Moving the left lever shifts you to the next higher or lower gear. Moving the right lever gives you a two-gear jump higher or lower.

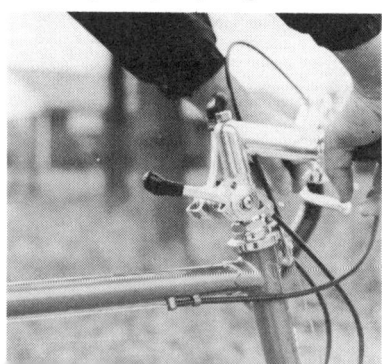

First, second, and third are the low gears. They serve for uphill starts and in hilly and mountainous areas where you need the extra power or leverage to make it to the top.

You don't have to start a ten-speed in first gear. Find the gear you prefer. It may be second or third. The higher the gear, the harder it is to pedal; that's why you use low gears for starting. If your feet spin too much as you start, or pedaling is too easy, shift to a higher gear.

For the lowest possible gear and maximum pedaling power, the chain goes on the *largest* cog in the rear. The right gear lever is pulled toward you as far as it will come. The chain goes on the *smaller* sprocket up front. The left lever is pushed forward as far as possible. The gear ratio, using a 14-17-20-24-28 (teeth) rear cog and a 48-52 (teeth) double-sprocket crank, is called a 46.

That's always derived by multiplying together the rear-wheel diameter (usually 27 inches) and the number of front-sprocket teeth, then dividing that by the number of rear-cog teeth. Hence 27 times 48, divided by 28, comes out to a 46 gear.

Second gear is also low. To set it, keep the right lever in the same fully back position. Move the left lever down. You'll feel the chain click onto the larger front sprocket. You need second gear for hills that are steep but not bad enough for first gear. How can you tell? Your feet seem to spin too much; pedaling is too easy. Maintain this principle: Shift to a higher gear when pedaling feels too easy.

To shift from second gear to third is a double shift. The chain needs to go back on the smaller front sprocket, and onto the second-largest rear cog. Pull the left lever toward you to make the first shift. The instant after you feel the chain set on the small sprocket, move the right lever to the next position upward. (Remember, this sequence applies only to bikes with sprockets close together in diameter. A 39-52 sprocket gives a different shift sequence.)

You can calculate the "gear" for second and third. For second, 27 times 52, divided by 28, comes to 50. Third gear: 27 times 48, divided by 24, which makes a "gear" of 54. Pedaling 60 turns a minute, you travel 8 mph in first gear, 9 mph in second, and a bit over 9½ mph in third.

CHART A GEARS ON 48/52 MULTISPEED BICYCLE				CHART B GEARS ON 39/52 MULTISPEED BICYCLE		
REAR COG ↓ / FRONT SPROCKET →	LARGER (LEVER DOWN)	SMALLER (LEVER UP)	REAR COG ↓ / FRONT SPROCKET →	LARGER (52 TEETH)	SMALLER (39 TEETH)
LARGEST (LEVER FULLY DOWN)	2ND (50 GEAR)	1ST (46 GEAR)	LARGEST (28 TEETH)	3RD (50 GEAR)	1ST (38 GEAR)
NEXT LARGEST (LEVER SECOND UP)	4TH (59 GEAR)	3RD (54 GEAR)	NEXT LARGEST (24 TEETH)	5TH (59 GEAR)	2ND (44 GEAR)
MIDDLE (LEVER MIDPOSITION)	6TH (70 GEAR)	5TH (65 GEAR)	MIDDLE (20 TEETH)	7TH (70 GEAR)	4TH (53 GEAR)
NEXT TO SMALLEST (LEVER FOURTH UP)	8TH (83 GEAR)	7TH (76 GEAR)	NEXT TO SMALLEST (17 TEETH)	9TH (83 GEAR)	6TH (62 GEAR)
SMALLEST (LEVER FULLY UP)	10TH (100 GEAR)	9TH (93 GEAR)	SMALLEST (14 TEETH)	10TH (100 GEAR)	8TH (75 GEAR)

Fourth, fifth, sixth, and seventh gears are for general riding. The charts below should guide you in figuring out gears and positions of the levers on your bike. Shift patterns differ radically.

More important is that you learn the "feel" of gear ratios with your legs. The two primary rules are: (1) WHEN PEDALING GETS TOO EASY, seek a HIGHER gear. You want to keep pedal pressure at about what's normal for you, without regard to the speed you're moving (unless you're in a race). (2) WHEN PEDALING GETS TOO HARD, seek a LOWER gear. Your normal pedal pressure can take you up steep hills. Learn to "feel out" the right gear.

Fourth "gear" in our example figures out to 58.5, and delivers an average 60-turns-per-minute speed around 10½ mph. Fifth "gear" is 65 (still using the formula on page 63); speed is about 11½ mph. Remember, though, it's pedal pressure you set the gears for, not mph. Fifth and sixth are your "normal" gears, for along-the-street riding. Sixth "gear" is 70, and spins you along at 12½ mph.

Seventh gear in the 48-52 machine is for fast cruising, with a gear of 76 (it's for normal riding in a 39-52 bike, with a gear of 70—chart B). This gear takes extra pedal effort. If you're in a hurry and have strong legs, 80 crank-turns a minute can roll you 18 mph. (Tenth gear delivers almost 18 mph at 60 pedal turns per minute, but takes quite a bit more pedal pressure.)

Eighth, ninth, and tenth are high gears. Some cyclists seldom use them. High gears are used for racing, for going downhill (so your pedals don't "run away" with you), or riding with strong wind at your back. Naturally, eighth gear is the more useful of the three in moderate riding situations. It has a "gear" of 82.5, and 60 pedal-turns a minute takes you 14¾ mph.

Ninth gear has a number of 92.5, and develops a speed of 16.5 mph. But pedal pressure begins getting heavy if you're trying it on level terrain.

The smallest rear cog and the larger front sprocket join forces to create tenth gear. It's the highest gear and is used by the average rider only for downhill. It has a "gear" of 100, and 18 mph just about coincides with 60 turns a minute of the crank.

You can buy a ten-speed bicycle with other cog sizes, to give different gear spreads. Or you can get smaller sprockets. As a possible-case example, a 39-45 sprocket and 14-18-22-28-34 cog gives a wide gear spread, from 30 to 86. Speed would range from a top of 15 to a low barely above 5 mph; but you could ride up a mountain with a machine geared that low.

There are practical limits, but you can order a bicycle tailored to your needs.

A five-speed bike has only one gear lever, the right-side one. It controls the derailleur at the rear hub where gear changes take place. You pedal with the gears on a five-speed very much like on a ten-speed. There are simply fewer gears to deal with. You're concerned with one lever instead of two.

A multispeed bike should always be moving when you shift. You don't exert heavy pressure on the pedals, although be sure they are rotating. Moving the lever all the way forward (away from you) gives the highest or fifth gear. You'll hear the gear click and know it has engaged. You'll also notice the difference in pedaling. From that, you can tell if you have engaged the correct gear.

You'll find uses for all the gears on a five-speed. The gear ranges are usually lower, because five-speeds are generally heavier bicycles, although still in the lightweight class. Each gear is further separated in "power," too, than in a ten-speed.

The front sprocket of some popular five-speed models carries 46 teeth. The rear-hub cog assembly typically has 14, 17, 21, 26, and 32 teeth. That gives an 85 fifth gear, 70 fourth, 56 third, 46 second, and 37 first.

That first gear is really low and powerful; you won't use it except for very steep hill-climbing. It's slow, too. A normal 60 crank-turns per minute moves the bike (on 26-inch tires) only 6½ mph. Third and fourth gears, the ones you'll use most, transport you at 10 and 12½ mph, respectively. Fifth or high gear moves you 15 mph or better.

As with any geared bicycle, the secret lies in knowing when to shift. The rules for a five-speed are the same as for a ten-speed. When your pedaling seems too easy, shift to a higher gear. You can slow the pedaling down if you don't want to go so fast; don't try to use the gears to control speed. And, when pedaling becomes labored, shift to a lower gear. You'll learn to feel the need in your legs.

Don't make the mistake of trying to shift a five-speed across two gears at a time. This can foul your derailleur. (It would do the same to a ten-speed if you jumped two cogs at once with the rear derailleur). You can shift fast enough without that. Just shift down (or up) one step with the lever. You should feel the shift take place more than hear it, if the derailleur is in good shape. It only takes a second or so. Then move the lever to the next position up or down, and wait for that shift to occur. You can avoid unnecessary maintenance and repairs.

In case you've forgotten the principles of bicycle gearing: First or low gear has the chain running over the smallest gear in the rear-hub cog assembly. That gives your pedals the most leverage, but turns the rear wheels the least for each pedal revolution. Shifting to higher gears moves the chain progressively to larger cogs. Third gear finds the chain on the middle cog, and fifth (high) gear on the largest one, next to the rear-wheel spokes. There, you get the most wheel travel per pedal revolution.

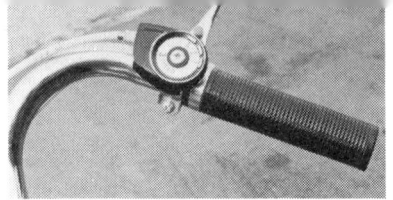 

A three-speed bicycle doesn't allow a wide choice of gears. You have low, medium, or high. But you shift about the same. You go by pedal pressure to signal the need for a change in gear ratio. If you're not exerting much pressure, and your feet can spin the pedals too easily, shift into a higher gear. When pedaling becomes something of an effort, more than is normal for you, shift into a lower gear.

The mechanism that shifts a three-speed is all contained inside the rear hub. It's called a *hub gear.* A sort of mechanical switch lever sticking out on the chain side of the hub does the shifting. You control it by cable from a small shift pod that mounts near your right handgrip. There's only one sprocket at the crank, and one cogwheel at the hub.

Ordinarily, you start out in low or first gear. That gives you extra leverage, and is especially useful if you have to start out on an upgrade. Shift to second once you have a bit of momentum.

Second (intermediate or medium) gear corresponds roughly with the regular drive of a single-speed bicycle. The gearing represents a compromise between speed and power.

Third or high gear has little power, but lets you pedal more slowly as you go faster.

Without a derailleur hanging on the rear hub, the three-speed bike offers less risk of costly damage. But don't flop it down on its right side, either. Use the kickstand, or lay it down gently on the left side.

Chapter 5

Around Home: Safe City Riding

Bicycling is meant to be fun. It can become tragic if you don't obey traffic laws and work toward safe riding. As more bicycles appear on the road, it seems more people pay no attention to courteous and sensible riding practices.

On your bike, you're subject to the same laws that govern motor traffic. Some bike riders don't realize this, or pretend they don't. They breeze through red lights, ignore stop signs, and even pay no attention to speed limits. You need to be particularly alert around a city. Your safety and the welfare of others depend on sane riding practices. They should be automatic with you.

You can receive a ticket for violating traffic laws on a bicycle the same as in a car. The police department in some areas conducts safety classes for cyclists who get tickets. Laws for bicycles vary slightly in different cities and states, but they closely resemble motor vehicle laws. Some cities require licensing and registering your bike. Check with your local police department or bicycle club.

Some police departments sponsor bike safety or inspection programs, often at a local school. However you manage it, learn to ride safely in your city.

Let's go over some basic rules and situations. Drivers are required to signal turns. Cyclists have the same responsibility. You as a cyclist are more vulnerable than a motorist. Severe injury to you and damage to your bike can result from failing to let other traffic know which way you're headed. Even when there seems to be no traffic, make hand signals for stops or turns.

When riding, you should be on the right side of the road. Handle left turns basically the same as if you were driving a car. A left turn on a bike requires extra caution, though. Come to a near-stop. Make your left-turn signal: ARM STRAIGHT OUT. Now check both behind and in front of you. Look to the right and left before you turn. If the way is clear and no car or other traffic has slipped up on you, proceed with your turn.

A car may come up behind you or next to you. You have the right-of-way to complete your left turn. But don't always count on that. The driver may not treat you as equal although legally you are. Figure out what he plans to do. If he comes alongside, cutting you off from the lane you need for turning, he most likely will ignore your hand signal. Stay out of his way.

When making some left turns, you cross lines of traffic. Wait for oncoming vehicles. The way must be clear before you can legally turn left.

Traffic from side streets (left and right) can't be trusted. You don't have to be quite as concerned if there are traffic lights. But even when cross-street traffic is supposed to stop, be on the alert. You and your bike may not be noticed. Particularly beware of hidden traffic on cross-streets that don't have traffic lights or stop signs. Hedges, buildings, and parked cars often cut off your view of side-street traffic. Edge out enough to see the traffic lanes. If the way is clear, make your hand signal, check behind you, and turn.

Whenever you make the left-turn signal, hold your left arm out long enough to be seen. A quick wave is hard to interpret. Keep it out until you are sure the way is clear for you to proceed.

You may be traveling on a four-lane street in the city and want to make a left turn. Part of the danger lies in getting into the left lane. Anticipate your turn in plenty of time to move over into the center lane at least 200 feet before you reach the intersection.

Watch for cars behind you as you start to change lanes. Make the left-turn hand signal. Get over. Now stay close to the center strip. When you arrive at the intersection, proceed as you would for any left turn. Remember, you have two lines of oncoming traffic to worry about, so watch out.

Right turns are less dangerous than the left turn, mainly because you don't cross any lanes of traffic. Your main concern is traffic on the street you're turning into. Check it right and left. If the traffic on that street has to stop for a sign, you can proceed after it comes to a stop. For greatest safety, don't make a right turn without checking all lanes of traffic.

If you're turning right from a stop street, check what the motorist behind is about to do. Even without a right-turn signal flashing, he may turn right. He could turn the corner short—right over you. With a left signal on, he might still turn right. Don't take anything about motorists for granted when you're out on a bike. They just don't watch for bicycles. Watch for oncoming car traffic that is making left turns. Staying as far to the right as possible keeps you at least partly out of the way of unexpected turns by automobiles.

To signal a right turn, hold your left arm straight out to the elbow and POINT THE FOREARM UPWARD.

Do not extend your right arm. Always use your left arm for signaling. It's more visible. Use your right arm to control your bicycle.

WRONG

A motorist has braking lights to signal that he's slowing down. As a cyclist you do not. Traffic following has no way of knowing when you plan to slow down or stop. You must hand-signal.

Stretch out your arm as for turns, except POINT YOUR FOREARM DOWNWARD. Use this slowing or stopping signal anywhere you slow your speed, such as at railroad tracks and intersections. Use your stop signal even though the whole line of traffic you're in knows to stop.

You are as obligated to wait for a red traffic light to turn green as a motorist is. You must obey stop signs, too. Violators pay fines. Worse, you might cause an accident by surprising a car which has the right-of-way. Even with a stop sign or light to direct you, check all traffic before you cross or turn.

Be prepared to stop at all times. City traffic is temperamental. Anticipate the unexpected. A panic stop might skid you into traffic or make you lose balance. Be especially alert when roads are slippery with rain, snow, or dew.

Exercise special caution at four-way stops. Most motorists don't acknowledge the rights a cyclist has. You should be allowed to turn or proceed when your turn comes. Go ahead and start, but watch to see if any cars have started out-of-turn. If they have, let them through. Be alert and alive, rather than hospitalized with the right-of-way.

Road conditions affect your stopping. You don't need to limit yourself to dry streets and good weather. You can ride in practically every condition if you and your bike are ready for it.

When stopping on wet pavement, or at an intersection strewn with gravel or sand, allow more distance for braking. If you don't, you might skid, fall, or not be able to stop in time to miss traffic. Traveling downhill multiplies the danger.

You have even less friction on ice or snow. They give you worse problems on a bike than in a car. Pump the brakes lightly instead of pulling hard on them. You'll come nearer stopping. Be especially careful around intersections. Even though *you* may not need to stop, a car might slide through. Test your brakes lightly before you get there. Don't ever wait, even on dry streets, until you are at an intersection to brake.

There's a drag when riding in snow that makes pedaling an extra effort. Be especially cautious at intersections where snow has melted and formed ice. Stopping in snow is always dangerous. Wear sunglasses. Glare hinders your ability to see.

Spring and summer, which are prime times for bicycling, bring unexpected showers. Freshly wet roads are deceptively slippery. Test your brakes after you ride through puddles and rain. The shoes may get wet; pumping the brakes heats and helps dry them. Watch out for chuckholes hidden under puddles of water.

Wet roads become more dangerous in autumn, because of leaves. An early morning frost can also create slippery lanes. Slow down enough that you can brake gently.

Learn to watch for several dangers at railroad crossings. First of all, you can't always trust an automatic signal that should come on when a train approaches. A circular yellow sign warns you when tracks are near. Some tracks use no automatic signal but instead have a crossed-arm wooden sign. This type is also preceded by the round yellow road sign. A railroad crossing might have a stop sign, so obey that too.

Stop at all railroad crossings, sign or no. Look both ways before you cross any track. Be especially cautious at a double track. Don't rush out as soon as a train passes. A second train may be coming and you might not hear it. Don't trust the schedule of trains in your area; they change.

Most railroad crossings are rough. Even a car gets jolted. Your multispeed bicycle is more delicate and susceptible to harm than a car. Crossing railroad tracks without stopping or slowing down can knock the wheels out of line, warp rims, bend spokes, and cause tires to go flat quickly (especially sew-ups). Take the time to stop completely. Then get off and walk your bike across the tracks. Careful bike owners carry their lightweight bikes across. Also, tracks are slippery and might cause a fall. Walking that few yards might avert an injury.

If you watch cyclists for a while, you'll see some inexperienced neophytes riding on the left side of the road as if they were walking. DON'T you do that. You ride on the far righthand side. The law says you must ride on the right. Ride a bike by the rules you would use to drive a car. For example, you never enter a one-way street except in the legal direction.

Ride a constant distance from the edge of the road rather than veering back and forth. Don't depend on your ears to anticipate traffic behind you. If you ride steadily, a car can pass you safely. Don't get so close to the edge that you wobble and lose balance. Rough shoulders damage tires and wheel alignment. And don't ever ride down the middle between lanes of traffic; that's suicide.

Riding in groups has advantages. Motorists are more likely to notice you. It's handy to have someone with you if an accident occurs.

You should ride single file in a group. Cyclists block traffic when they ride several abreast, and motorists get rightly perturbed. Don't follow the cyclist in front of you closely. He may have to stop suddenly without signaling. If you have to stop, do your best to signal the cyclist behind. Be careful when passing another cyclist. Consider the bike following you as well as the one you're passing.

If you're riding with two or more, cross streets and make turns separately. Do the same at stop streets. Groups have a mistaken tendency to cross intersections in bunches. This is dangerous anywhere, but especially in the city. Very large groups sometimes have police escorts for city riding. In that case you do cross and turn as a group.

Pedaling beside a truck or semitrailer is dangerous. The driver probably can't see you. Most trucks keep to the rightmost lane, the same lane cyclists use. Large trucks don't leave much room, even for skinny bicycles. Some roads don't have shoulders; that and curbs could block you off.

If a truck comes up beside you, slow down until he passes. Bad weather brings more danger. In snow, sleet, or rain, you might not slide but the truck might. Stay behind rather than beside.

Avoid getting caught between cars. If you find yourself in this situation, use hand signals and get to the right side as soon as possible. Don't follow closely; a car may stop without warning.

Traveling down alleys can be perilous. The space for passing a car is snug. The main danger is at the end. You have to anticipate pedestrians and autos out there since you can't see them. Slow down near the end. Stop and look before you cross the sidewalk or enter the street.

Keep in mind that storekeepers put trash in alleys. Look out for metal and glass.

You owe pedestrians the right-of-way, usually. When they're around, be prepared to stop suddenly if someone steps into your path. You can't always see pedestrians. Along a row of parked cars, someone might pop out in front of you suddenly (page 15). You could hit him, swerve into traffic, or skid and fall. A door swinging open can hit you. Watch for parked cars entering traffic. Watch near the ground underneath parked cars for the feet of playing children. City riding demands alertness and concentration.

Stunts look exciting. But you ask for trouble when you play on traveled streets.

Your bike holds one person only, unless you have a child seat. Balance changes and becomes difficult with someone on handlebars, luggage frame, or top tube. Someone on the handlebars obstructs your view. Two passengers also strains the bike. Finally, it's illegal.

A common stunt is riding hands-off. A cyclist needs to be ready for the unexpected. You may need both hands to avert an accident with a quick swerve. Carrying packages in your arms gives you the same disadvantage. Use bags or baskets for parcels.

Don't weave back and forth on the road as if you're waltzing. A motorist may not realize what you're doing or where you're going. And if he's not alert, you may swing right into his path.

It's also dangerous to race in traffic. You can't react soon enough to danger. And thinking about winning leads you to take chances you'd otherwise know better than to try. You may fail to notice an approaching car, a stoplight, or a hidden pedestrian. Stopping is difficult at high speed. If you want to race, read Chapter 8 and do it right.

You may choose to do your city riding on bike routes. They are set up, theoretically, to follow safe and scenic streets and roads. Signs guide you out of congested areas to suburbs and rural locales. Some routes wind through parks. Departments of Transportation and Departments of Parks and Recreation lay out better routes if they work with local bike clubs. You can obtain bicycling maps from these departments, from your Chamber of Commerce, or from the bike clubs. They're usually free.

Time yourself following bike routes. You can travel about 10 miles in an hour. Most maps have miles marked. Remember to add the miles you must ride to the route's starting point. Divide the total distance by ten; that tells you how many hours of cycling you're in for.

Take a watch along so you can determine how far to travel and leave time to return. When half your allotted time is gone, head back. If your bike route circles, you'll have to calculate. You may ride slower going home, too.

If you forget your watch, estimate time by the sun. Listen for local time signals such as factory whistles or church chimes. Lots of villages have a noon whistle. Courthouses in small towns often have a clock in the dome. Many banks display time and temperature.

Most bikes come with basic safety items. A used bike may not have them.

Back reflectors and front light are required for night riding. You can buy battery-operated lights that fasten to your arm. They're enough in Europe, but U.S. laws demand a light attached to the bike. An extra light on your arm enables a motorist to spot you better. Make yourself easier to see at night by adding reflective tape to fenders and other parts of your bike. Some pedals have reflectors. You can attach reflectors to the spokes.

Safety flags attract a motorist's attention in daytime. They are not just a fad. Your bike should be visible to motorists and to other cyclists. Bright paint colors help. Wear light-colored clothing. You can buy parkas and jackets that are brightly colored *and* reflective at night. For daytime, wear clothes with contrasting colors: two-tone jackets, backpacks, and bike bags. You may see cycling shoes with Scotchlite reflective tape, or even with round glass reflectors fastened to the backs of the heels. Safety applies 24 hours a day.

Chapter 6

Crosscountry Pedaling Trips

Bicycles offer a fascinating form of vacation and recreation. Cyclists nowadays think nothing of traveling clear across the country.

A bike vacation may sound tiring and impossible to you. It is, if you take off without previous riding experience. Chances are, if you really like cycling, you'll pretty soon be planning longer journeys with your bike.

Bike clubs sponsor relatively short tours—100 miles or so. These only take a weekend. A few clubs sponsor biking vacations. The League of American Wheelmen magazine publicizes tours that are open to almost anyone. The most popular tours cover scenic areas of the country.

Individuals plan bicycling vacations and invite friends to join them. Others go it alone. That's not a good idea unless you know how to route a tour. Unfamiliar areas constitute the problem. Hearing about other cyclist's journeys might help you decide where to go and what roads to avoid.

Figure out how much time you have. From experience you know how far you can go in a day. Unfamiliar byways and unexpected road conditions will slow you down some. And allow time for browsing around.

Departments of Transportation in many states have scenic or historic bike trips already routed. You could connect several such routes to extend length. Write to bike clubs in states you want to visit, to see what they have routed out already.

Traveling by bicycle instead of a car lets you see more of any locality. You discover places cars don't usually get to. The view you get of a region is more realistic and complete.

You meet people along the road and at stops. Strike up conversations. Small towns have a history and the natives love to share it. They'll direct you to local points of interest. The people you meet may even *be* the main points of interest.

Part of your fun may come from discovering as you ride. Stop and investigate whatever looks interesting. Linger in out-of-the-way places. Some cyclists *never* stop at the regular tourist attractions.

Most of us don't really know our own states. Bicycling slows you down enough to see. A three-day weekend can take you to exciting places you've never paid the slightest attention to. Read the newspaper for events within riding distance that you'd like to attend. Take off for a new area and explore it on your own.

You'll eventually be lured to other states. Seasoned cyclists don't let even a thousand-mile stretch stop them. Cycling brings vacationing a new dimension.

Bicycles are not allowed on the interstate highways. Seldom are they the most direct route to your destination, anyway. Besides, scenic country roads happen to be one of the attractions of bicycling. Winding roads and nature's sounds offer a quiet change from city bustle.

You'll be surprised at the small things you see and notice. You can watch animals going about their business. Cross-country riding satiates you with fresh air and exercise. A day of pedaling almost invariably assures you of a good night's sleep. You'll likely wake up full of energy.

Expenses are small, bicycling. If you camp, you save on everything—including food expense. Although all these benefits are significant, most cross-country cyclists do it because they enjoy it for itself.

Touring alone isn't any more difficult than touring with a group, if you've toured before. Don't tackle it without experience. Otherwise, follow the same procedures you would for group touring. You might want to call home every couple of days to reassure someone of your safety and whereabouts. (Carry dimes for toll phones.) Camping alone isn't always safe, but that doesn't mean to exclude it definitely. Do your own thing on your bike!

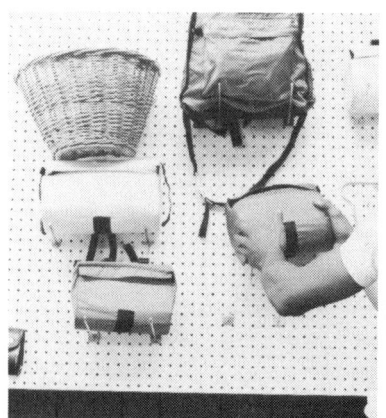

If you use your bike for traveling, you need bags. *Panniers* fit on either side of the rear wheel. They are large enough to hold more items than a rear bag (behind the saddle) or a front bag (in front of the handlebars). A backpack that's comfortable can replace bike bags or supplement them. Don't get "bagged" down. The touring cyclist needs to keep light.

Waterproof nylon bags keep things dry if you get caught in a rainstorm. Some bags have linings that zip out to be washed. Bright-colored bags make you more visible to motorists.

When buying bags, think *quality.* Nylon bags with removable linings are the more expensive. But if you do much touring, commuting, or traveling to school on your bike, the added cost pays off. Better bags attach securely to the bike with nylon straps. Leather straps tend to stretch; exposed to rain, dew, and sun, leather also cracks and rots.

Some panniers zip together off the bike, forming one bag that is convenient to tote.

Each person has his own method of packing a suitcase. Packing bike bags is the same, except it requires even more thought and foresight. Well-organized packing makes finding items easier when you need them. Repacking is quicker, too. Some bags have outside pockets to hold small loose items like toothbrushes and nail clippers. These are items that otherwise require digging around to find.

One packing method works rather well. Spread out on the floor everything you want to take. Group items together according to how often you'll be using them. Assess carefully which things you can possibly do without. Put them in a group of their own. Later, if there's a spare corner (or a spare pound of weight), you can include them. Otherwise, out they go. If you want to take along your camera or a large notebook, you may have to sacrifice something else. The primary idea is to pack light. You don't want to be lugging more than about 30 lb with you, or you'll become very weary of hauling it.

Next, divide the group of little-used items and place some of them in the bottom of each bag. Then on top of those, in both bags, come the items you'll be using more often. Finally, on top, you place things you must have access to several times a day.

Clothes, for example, can be packed into small plastic bags —a day's worth in each. Then you needn't mix dirty clothes with clean ones as you use them. Plan each day's wardrobe. Place the clothes for the end of the trip at the bottom, ones you'll use soon on top.

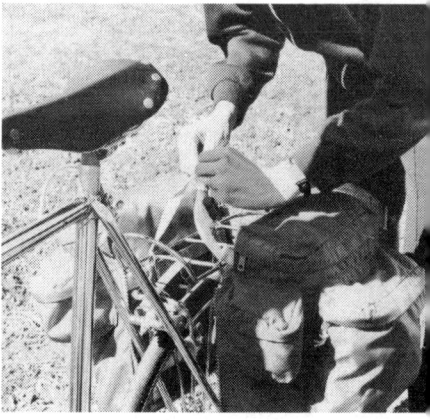

Use the front bag of your bicycle for maintenance items. You can cushion tools by packing them between clothes. Or, buy a compact set of bike tools that fits in its own small bag below the saddle. Take a tire-patching kit. A spare inner tube helps some cyclists feel more secure. You want mechanical independence when you travel long distances without auto support. Cyclists have come up with ingenious ways to nurse a bike on to a town for repairs.

Take a chain tool and several links. A tire pump that attaches to the rear bike tube is handy for touring. You need a pressure gauge too. A bit of lubricating oil is wise. Other handy items include a knife, first-aid kit, small (lightweight) flashlight, compass, sunglasses, mechanical pencil and leads, paper (airmail), maps, credit cards, and cash. When a group travels, you can share the first-aid kit, maps, and anything else you can figure out.

Don't pack things you can buy as you travel. Touring doesn't mean stranding yourself from civilization. Pack some energy foods for breaks, but not much; you can replenish your supply every day or so. Most energy foods are compact. Dried fruit won't spoil quickly.

Use every bit of space. You won't find any miracle method of packing. Tuck things in where they fit best. Packing bags isn't difficult; you just don't have a lot of extra room.

The typical touring setup consists of front and rear bags. The smaller bag fits in back since a large bag would get in your way swinging on and off the bike. Some tourists, who don't like the way front bags affect steering, prefer panniers which fit low astride the back.

If you stay at youth hostels or motels, you don't have to worry about sleeping equipment. You might want to take along cooking equipment, though. It all depends on the kind of touring you do and the type of traveling you enjoy.

Make a list and check things off. Try to keep the weight of your baggage under 30 lb. Try for 25. The further you travel, the more difference the extra weight makes. And if you have under 25 lb, don't look for something more to take!

You'll develop the most suitable way to load your bicycle. The photos on the facing page illustrate how one frequent tourist loads hers. Note the definite sequence. Practice in your backyard if this is your first tour.

After a few tours, you'll learn how few clothes you really need. You'll use much less space in your bike bags for clothes. Beginners almost always take too much, unless a veteran cyclist has helped them pack.

Comfort is one key to what you wear and take along. For summer riding, shorts and sleeveless shirts are comfortable. Knits seem better for the cyclist than other fabrics. They fold up tight, don't wrinkle much, and wash and dry quickly. Riding gloves protect hands from blisters and numbness. (You can make cycling gloves by cutting off the fingers of old gloves.)

When you dress too warm, too cold, or in ill-fitting clothes, riding becomes unbearable. Riding, like any exercise, warms you. Even on cool days you don't have to dress as heavily as you might expect. Dress so you can take off extra layers if necessary. Start out wearing a lightweight jacket. Athletic warmup suits use the layered principle: shorts underneath loose-fitting warmup pants. Allow space in your bags for jackets or sweaters you might remove.

You need only one or at most two changes of clothes. You can launder them on long trips. Take a long-sleeve shirt, and an extra short-sleeve shirt. Shorts don't get in your way pedal-

ing. Fall touring may require slacks rather than shorts. You can buy clips which hold the slacks close to your leg.

A word of advice. Don't wear anything new when you tour. Break in new clothes by wearing them around the house and laundering them several times.

When it rains, cyclists ride right on. That's one reason waterproof bags are good to have. Few touring cyclists would take along an umbrella, so they ride with no protection at all. Some enjoy a rainstorm, in a perverse way. Others take plastic rain capes. Even if you get wet, knits and synthetics dry quickly in warm wind and sun.

In a thunderstorm or an extremely hard rain, ask a farmer if you can wait in his barn until the storm passes. You can get under a bridge or in a large culvert. But DON'T take cover under a tree. In a heavy electrical storm, with thunder and lightning, you're safer lying flat in a ditch than just about anywhere.

Cyclists with plenty of stamina take breaks only when it's time to eat. Others enjoy the breaks as much as the cycling. When you're with a group, and the ride has been planned, breaks are usually set for every so-many miles. They are spotted near restrooms and places to buy snacks. Some leaders stop and give the group a break when beginning a new part of the tour. A very large group splits conveniently into several smaller ones, leaving each group on its own to stop whenever necessary. You'll find restroom facilities at roadside rest areas, in parks, in restaurants, in gasoline stations.

Even the most rugged cyclist needs an occasional break. Don't push yourself or your fellow riders. When you tire, stop and rest. Some club groups make it a practice to break every 10 to 15 miles. You can travel farther and remain in better spirits if you stop now and then. Work your breaks around visiting some point of interest or checking maps for more directions.

Take a longer break in the middle of your riding day to rest. On a 100-mile ride, a long break at around 50 miles divides the day nicely. The best breaks just happen, when you see something interesting, or meet someone to talk with.

Feet can have it rough on a bicycle tour. Some people develop blisters even on short rides. Blisters are almost always a problem on your first big tour, if you haven't been building up to the long ride gradually.

If you don't wear cycling shoes, wear sneakers or a similar shoe. Cycling shoes have a metal support in the sole that helps you pedal easier and keeps your foot from cramping through overexercise. Wear shoes that are well broken-in when you cycle. Sandals may seem like a good idea for summer riding, but they're not. Neither is cycling barefoot. Whatever shoes you wear, include socks. They help your sweaty feet "breathe." They also cushion your foot and help prevent blisters.

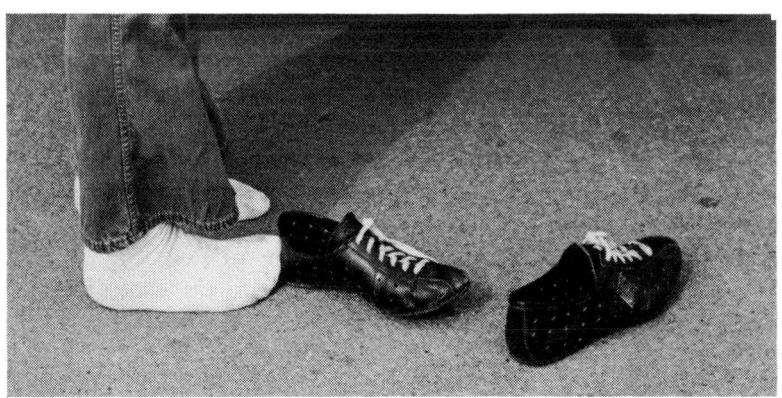

Eating shouldn't be much of a problem. If you camp, you can take "instant" foods or freeze-dried foods, or buy supplies the day you need them. Even if you don't camp, you may want to buy supplies at a grocery and cook them yourself. Restaurants abound, and you can meet some interesting people in small-town eating places. Certain restaurants become regular stopping places for touring groups. Fast-food chains are all over the place. Vary your eating. Mix camping, picnicking, and restaurants.

Avoid overeating. Smaller meals, and more often, do best for most cyclists. Exercising after heavy eating can make you sick. Plan a longer break around your largest meal. Riding a bike doesn't need to change your eating habits drastically, although many cyclists feel best when they eat moderately. Try three light meals and several high-energy snacks like raisins, fruit, nuts, or health-food-type grain mixtures.

If your bike doesn't have a water tank on it (page 99), by all means get one before you start touring. You lose a lot of water through perspiring, and you can't count on being near a water supply when thirst strikes. Water can refresh you more than a snack. Remember to refill the tank at restaurants and when taking breaks at parks or gas stations.

Taking a vacation on your bike or touring for more than a day requires some kind of sleeping arrangements. When groups travel, motel reservations can be arranged by the sponsoring club. Your group might rather take along sleeping bags and arrange for a place to camp.

If you're making plans for yourself, estimate how far you want to go in one day. Some cyclists travel leisurely, others at a faster pace. If you tour with children, you have to consider their capabilities. A range of 50 to 90 miles is typical. Don't plan a tour of more than a few days without having several shorter jaunts under your belt. They'll help you estimate your average distance per day. Then you can decide where to make reservations. Route yourself through cities that have accommodations. Leave your itinerary with a friend or relative so you can be reached in an emergency.

Overnight camping facilities are often harder to find than motels. Your sleeping bag is the only equipment you need, or a small tent. Some city parks allow overnight stays; most do not. Farmers are hesitant to permit impromptu camping—and don't try that without permission or you may find buckshot in your breakfast food. Camping organizations (like KOA) are your best bet. The one nearest you can usually help find others along your route.

When you camp or meander on the road, finding sleeping accommodations where and as you need them, getting in touch with you could be difficult. Call home (or a friend) now and then to let someone know where you are. A schedule of calls every second day or once a week is good protection. If you missed calling, due perhaps to some mishap, someone would know to start hunting for you. You can also apprise friends of changes in your schedule.

Finding a phone to call from shouldn't be difficult. Restaurants, laundromats, and motels have public phones, and there are lots of booths around—even in very small towns.

Chapter 7

Some Hints on Bicycle Camping

Off-the-road bicycling and camping often go together, but they don't have to. Many parks with camping facilities also have bike trails. Some city parks have unpaved trails that let you enjoy bicycling in a setting quieter than the city streets. You don't have to worry about cars and traffic. It's just you, your bike, and nature. You may see wildlife that you wouldn't see beside a traveled road. Keepers of bike trails often avoid using herbicides to clear the edges. Undergrowth and overgrowth are natural. The nature lover can feel at home on such trails. If you like solitude, this is it.

That's the kind of locale you should try to camp in. The camping itself can be a world of fun. But with natural bicycling trails just outside your tent flap, what more could you wish for?

There's some special pioneering thrill about combining a long bicycle tour with a camping trip. A world of cyclists are finding that camping with a bike isn't nearly as complicated as it may sound. Try an overnight camp-out at home or within a few miles. This experience, however brief, helps you decide what to take along and what you can get by without. You'll also find whether or not you really enjoy camping. It's not everyone's bag.

Try nearby state parks next. Some city parks offer camping facilities and bike trails. Any place within a day's journey serves your get-acquainted purpose. Write your state's Department of Recreation for information about parks.

Consider national parks for camping. This gives you a chance to see more of the United States and enjoy special parts of the country. Some don't permit bicycle camping, because of dangerous wildlife. Write the National Park Service, Washington DC 20240. Ask specifically for information on parks that have bike trails and bike-camping facilities.

When you're on long bicycling trips, you can occasionally find camping sites by knocking on farmers' doors and asking if they mind letting you camp overnight. Be meticulous, and do not leave the slightest trash. If you restore the area to exactly as you found it, you and others might be welcome later. Don't ever camp on farms or in roadside woods without first asking permission.

It is risky to camp without advance plans. You can't depend on local farmers to provide sites. Yet, you don't want to be stuck in the middle of nowhere with no place to sleep. In most states it's illegal to camp at roadside parks or along the side of the road. Even some state and local parks prohibit camping. Find out in advance of your long journey whether you can build a fire certain places or not, and if you need reservations or have to pay a fee.

You may have to travel extra distance some days to reach facilities that suit you. If time is at a premium, you might consider other transportation for you and your bike.

A cartop or rear-mounted bike caddy lets you haul up to six bikes. Don't feel that taking a car along ruins the idea of bike camping. It's a practical means of getting to a distant park where you can camp and ride along bike trails.

Some cyclists travel to takeoff points by plane, bus, or train. It depends on where you live and where you're headed. Many airlines, bus companies, and Amtrack ship bikes.

On buses, there's no extra charge if your bike is within normal luggage limits. Your bike must be dismantled and put in a container, which you provide. Take care that all parts are padded and that loose screws, bolts, and nuts won't be lost. Insure your luggage.

Airlines provide a shipping box, but you pay for it. Your bike doesn't need to be dismantled. The handlebars need to be turned inside. Airline personnel will crate your bike when you check in. It's therefore a good idea to arrive at the check-in counter an hour or two before departure.

Amtrack accepts bikes, but they load them as baggage, with no box protection. This can scratch your bike since you have no assurance it won't be mishandled. You can supply your own box or dismantle the machine and pack it for added protection.

Basically you take the same things for camping that you take touring. But overnighting adds a bit to your baggage. Of course, if you travel to a camping site by car, that solves most packing problems.

In addition to the clothes you normally take touring, include a pair of long slacks or jeans. They come in handy in the mountains or for chilly evenings. Trousers also protect your legs in rough brushy areas.

Take an extra jacket, warmer than your nylon one. You can wear both if it gets cold enough. A second long-sleeve shirt comes in handy for the same reason.

Take a pair of hiking shoes for when you aren't cycling. There will be places you'll want to walk to, and cycling shoes aren't comfortable for that. Too, it's good to let your cycling shoes air out at the end of the day's ride. Extra socks may be needed for warmth or if you stay far from a laundromat.

Food is a concern if you are camping far out in the wilderness. Sporting-goods stores carry freeze-dried and some instant foods. These packets cost more than food you might prepare from staples, but they're light and compact. You can carry a week's supply with no worry of spoilage. Most require mainly that you add water.

You may choose to buy each day's food supply at a grocery store along the way. That's what most cyclists do. Practically all organized camping facilities have a grocery store nearby that caters to picnickers and campers. Find out the store's hours or you could end up without a meal.

Water can be a problem. Most campsites and parks have water hydrants. You could use a collapsible canvas bucket to carry water in. A pan from your mess kit works, too. The water tank on your bike won't hold enough for cooking, cleaning, and drinking. If you isolate yourself when you camp, you may need to boil water from a nearby stream or take along water-purification tablets.

Absolutely do not forget a good first-aid kit. It can save your life—most especially if you're out alone. You can put your own together. Include roll gauze and pads, some square bandages, tape, Band-Aids, antiseptic, aspirin, suntan lotion, insect repellent, poison-ivy lotion, and scissors.

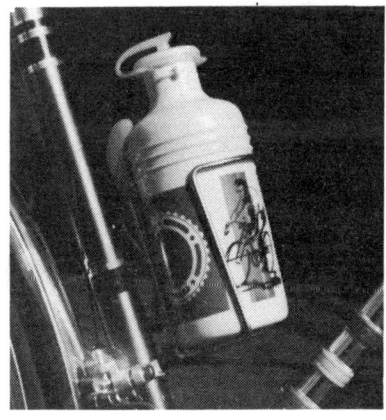

You need special compact camping equipment and supplies. One bulky item is your sleeping bag or tent. Down-filled sleeping bags are lighter, more compact, and warmer than other types. The high cost ($70 or more) pays off if you do much camping. Strap your sleeping bag firmly to the front or back of your bike, making sure it won't rub against the tires. Take trial rides to see how it affects your riding. You may want to shift its position.

You could prefer a tent. It offers more protection from rain. Pup tents are best. A piece of plastic stretched over homemade poles will do, too. If you travel in company, pick a size two can use. Share the carrying.

In addition to your trial campout before embarking on a longer trip, practice putting up the tent blindfolded—really. Dark comes too soon on some long rides. Don't wait until you're at your campsite to discover a stake missing.

Cooking equipment is a critical item. It can be heavy if you don't choose well. A small stove like backpackers use seems best. Backpackers and cyclists both need to keep things light. You can buy a tiny stove that has matching pots which fit on top (opposite page). You don't need a separate mess kit; eat from the pans. A compact cooking kit includes several pots which fit right into the largest. Lids convert to skillets. Put lightweight potholders between metal to quiet rattling.

Fuel for these small stoves poses no problems. Some use a replaceable fuel core. Others have refillable cores. Take along enough fuel.

Don't forget crucial items like can opener or matches. Drop matches into a plastic sandwich bag for protection from dampness. Soap pads are better for camping than dish soap.

Bicycle camping suits all ages. The expense of equipment may limit how extensively you camp, but once you've made the initial outlay the cost is cheaper by far than motels. You can learn to get along quite enjoyably without soft beds and warm showers.

Even bicycle afternoons can be turned into camping mini-jaunts. A few pots and pans, a tiny camp stove, and some food convert easily into a small campsite. But there are two cautions: One, don't do it in areas where camping and picnicking are forbidden. Second, be extremely careful of fires that might start from those small stoves. Clear the ground of leaves and sticks around the stove, to a circle at least 3 feet in diameter. Open cookfires are particularly dangerous. Campfires are for experienced woodsmen, and should be surrounded by a 10-foot circle of bare ground.

Equip yourself, practice a few times near home, and then take the plunge. Embark on bicycling's most nature-oriented pastime: camping.

(P.S. You can learn a wealth about safe, sane camping from *Forest H. Belt's Easi-Guide to Camping Comfort*.)

Chapter 8

If the Racing Bug Bites

Those who look on bicycling as a hobby often turn to racing. It's an exciting facet of a fun sport, and appeals mightily to the athletic and well coordinated individual. The cost is not intrinsically great. Yet, as you'll see in the next few pages, bicycle racing is not a sport to enter into lightly. There may be more to it than met your eye before now. At least, you can evaluate for yourself whether you want to get involved in that branch of bicycling activity.

Bicycle racing falls into three main categories: road races, criterium races, and track races. The most popular and common is the road race. The cyclists cover a distance of 40 to 100 miles. Road racing takes place on local streets, highways, and country roads. A course often includes urban and rural areas. Markers guide the racers.

In this type of race, the more experienced riders win. Experience teaches you to be alert for hidden sharp turns, oddly angling roads, loose horses, and slow-moving vehicles. Such varied road conditions challenge the racer. Falling in loose gravel a few times teaches you to watch for such things and handle them in future races.

Strategy counts in road racing. You must know your bike and its responses and vagaries. A mistake can injure you or batter your bike. Speed doesn't always decide a winner. Skill and endurance work for you until near the end. There, you'll make a concentrated effort at speed. This is called sprinting. If a cyclist leads all the way, but gets left behind in those last few yards—no win.

Road races are very long sometimes. A special road race in California not long ago covered 685 miles. There were starting and finishing points for each day. This kept the group together, rather than each entrant having to cover the entire distance on his own. Daily tabulations determined the final winner.

Cyclists usually can complete a road race in one day. Spectators line streets or roads where the racers will pass. In longer races, feed stations are set up. As the cyclist races past, a helper hands him quick-energy food or a drink.

The *criterium* (or criterion) race is second in popularity among cyclists. Criteriums bear similarities to road racing. The average criterium covers about 25 miles. A course is marked, and usually blocked off, around an area—for example, a city block. The racers repeat this course until they have ridden some preset number of miles.

Criteriums don't always remain in the city. This brand of racing draws more spectators, as a rule, than road racing. In criteriums, fans line the streets to watch and cheer their favorite riders as they pass again and again.

The third popular form of bicycle racing happens on tracks. Banked turns of 30 to 50 degrees allow high speed in short distances. The best tracks are paved.

Track racing involves numerous kinds of events. Individual and team competition multiply the variety. Time-trials, against a clock, emphasize how quickly a rider can go a measured distance. Sprint races place importance on getting over the finish-line before someone else.

The Little 500, a nationally known event that takes place at Indiana University, uses a track. This race, though popular, is a closed race. It is not connected with the Amateur Bicycle League of America, which sponsors most national competition. Spectator turnout corroborates the enthusiasm bicycle racing engenders.

What kind of person races? Seriousness and dedication mark good racers. A top competition rider has determination and is willing to sacrifice.

The racer acquires a mental attitude that's different from that of the "mere" bike lover. He enjoys competition. He practices discipline. Race riders thrive on the intensity a race incites. Physical condition means a lot. This entails training. An overweight, out-of-shape rider doesn't fit into racing. Muscle and machine become one entity in a race. Neither poor machine nor poor body wins races.

The serious racer needs a family for support. They usually haul him and his bike to competitions. They cheer him on, hand him food at feed stations, help him get bikes set up and ready. In races that allow it, they follow in a car with supplies, tools, and spare parts—even an extra bicycle.

He needs financial support, too. Without it, he can't spend enough time training. Even a part-time job interferes with racing. The most likely racer is a son or daughter whose family enjoys racing as much as the rider does.

The bicycle racer needs an exceptionally lightweight ten-speed machine. Light bikes cost more than others because of the alloy frame construction. Other alloy components are typical on a racing bike. A top racing machine can cost you $400 or more. Given equal experience and skill, the rider on the lighter bike wins the race. Even a few ounces can be critical. No effort is spared to keep the bike's weight down. You won't find any unnecessary items on a racer's bike. (There's more about lightweight bikes in Chapter 2.)

The tires on racing bikes are sew-ups, which weigh less because of the thin layers of rubber they're made of. Sew-ups decrease road resistance. Their high air pressure, over 100 psi, enables the racer to utilize his pedaling energy efficiently. Lightweight rims help make the bike responsive to the road and the rider.

Besides a light bike, some accessories help the racing competitor. Toe clips aid in proper pedaling (see *ankling* on page 57). A water tank attached to the front or head tube is a necessity. A racer's body loses huge amounts of water, which must be replaced.

Quick minor repairs are sometimes necessary. A sew-up flat takes much time to repair, so racers stockpile entire wheels in spots where road conditions might cause a blowout. The quick-release hub makes the switching quick, so riders can win despite such delays.

Cycling attire is standard. Reinforced shorts help cushion the uncomfortable racing seat. Cycling shoes secure a cyclist's feet in the toe clips. Cleats on the bottom of a racing shoe fit into the pedals. The foot nevertheless releases from the pedal in case of a fall. Cycling gloves protect hands. A padded crash helmet, constructed in strips for ventilation, protects the head in spills or accidents.

Racing jerseys display club or private colors. An elite racer may wear a silk jersey that is a prize received in another race. Silk, incidentally, offers less wind resistance than cotton or wool, and so is preferred by experienced racers.

All sports require training. Bicycle racing allows no exceptions. Racers like to train with other good racers. Each pushes and challenges the other. Winners often come from areas where one top racer influences many. His techniques and style are mimicked by those who train with him.

Imagine you're headed for racing. Here's a typical training day. You start out slowly in the morning for a half-hour. Then you push yourself almost to the limit for ten minutes, slow for ten, stop for five, then continue medium-strenuous pedaling. In the afternoon, you head for some hills and rough road surfaces. You ride up and down the same steep hill for two hours. In the evening, you meet some racing friends and run time trials for awhile against each other. You then have a quick sprint and head home for the day.

Good racers train the year around. Winter doesn't stop them, even though they may not ride outside. A racer can set his bike on rollers and pedal for hours inside. Cyclists in training ride the equivalent of 60 miles or so a day for four out of five days. They try to average about 20 mph. The more training and practice a cyclist engages in, the better his chances to win. And that's what the true racer lives for.

Besides riding, a bike racer can train other ways. Ice-skating uses many of the same muscles bicycling does. Moderate and planned weightlifting tones pedaling muscles and keeps them in shape.

Getting to a race can involve hundreds of miles. A racer needs lots of experience in competition to win state and national events. Local races don't happen frequently enough to offer this much competitive activity. Traveling becomes a way of life to the racer and his family. Riders from one area may pool resources and travel together in a van to cut expenses.

By the time you load extra tires, tools, food, and bikes, the trip to a race becomes an expedition. You have to prepare for a variety of conditions. You might get rain; the race goes on, and you'll want to use different tires. Some repair almost always becomes necessary. It's disheartening to journey 500 miles to race and not get to start because something's broken.

Racers have to "set up" their bikes before the race. Most bikes are dismantled for hauling, so you have to reassemble them. The qualified racer has also learned to be a mechanic. You pump up tires, check brakes, and correct wheel alignment. The careful racer gives his bike one quick last check for any minor maladjustments. Then he's ready to ride.

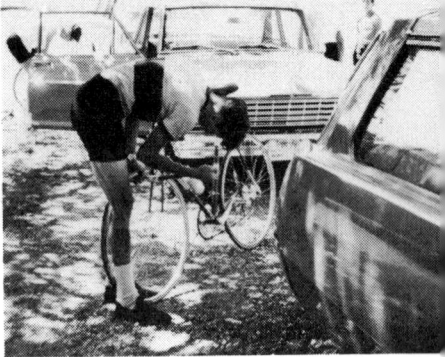

Racing cyclists ride within a few inches of each other. Wrecks do happen. Inexperience causes most of the bad ones. When one cyclist slides and falls, it often causes a chain reaction. The inexperienced rider can cause the experienced racer to lose or get hurt. Many clubs organize their races according to ability and age, thereby narrowing the problem somewhat.

A good racer walks over the course before he competes on it. You look for gravel and loose sand which may cause skidding. Chuckholes can damage your bike frame or cause a blowout. An unscrupulous competitor may even try to lead you deliberately into a chuckhole, causing you to lose speed. That's not possible if you remember where the bad spots are. These seemingly small impediments work against you when you're trying to win. The closeness of other cyclists prevents your seeing obstacles once you're racing. Memory can help a good rider win the race. Through experience, you learn to handle ticklish situations like these. You can avert catastrophes that tear up bikes and riders.

The bicycle racer competes against many of the same cyclists at race after race. Eventually, he knows what to expect from some of them. Bicycle racing involves more than taking off at the starting line and making it to the finish. The wise racer anticipates what lies ahead. A group may block him. Someone may try to lure or force him into a bad section of track or road. Positions switch back and forth.

In long races, cyclists tend to position themselves behind another cyclist. The follower benefits from the wind "tunnel" created by the front rider, decreasing his own wind resistance. You get the same effect on a freeway when you drive behind a large truck. Team members do this to help each other. This practice is called *drafting.* It lets a cyclist use less energy. That energy is needed for the last few-hundred yards.

And it's those final yards that count in most races. The riders have been taking it comparatively easy until then. As the finish looms, they concentrate all the force they can exert for one final burst of speed. This is *sprinting.* A rider who excels in distance stamina but can't sprint often finds himself the loser, unless his previous lead has grown very long.

Racers don't take home much money out of winning a bicycle race. Awards of value come in the form of merchandise contributed by local dealers for the publicity. Most of the goodies apply in some way to racing. A national winner receives a distinctive silk jersey he can wear in any races he's in the following year. The next most coveted awards are medals and trophies. However, the greatest reward of racing, the majority of competition riders agree, is the challenge of the duel—and of course the satisfaction of winning.

Racing isn't everyone's bag. If you're interested in it, you'll need to be licensed in order to compete. The Amateur Bicycle League of America sets up events that finally determine state and national champions. A license costing $5 entitles you to enter any amateur races that ABLA members sponsor. For information write: Amateur Bicycle League of America, P.O. Box 2175, New York NY 10017.

Chapter 9

Maintenance for Safety and Economy

A multispeed bicycle is an elaborate and expensive piece of machinery. Take care of it, and all those precision parts will operate the way they should. Neglect it, and your bike can become unsafe and a constant drain on your checkbook. Regular attention makes your bike last longer.

You don't have to be a mechanic. Simple maintenance can be handled with a kit of tools you can buy in almost any bike shop. The pouch includes a variety of wrenches and tire tools.

When something goes wrong with your bike, either fix it yourself or get it fixed immediately. Not only does a minor problem get worse—and more costly to repair—if you wait, but it can damage associated mechanisms. This chapter mentions most of the parts and assemblies on your bicycle. Once a week during the biking season you should examine each of them. The effort can save you money, and maybe injury.

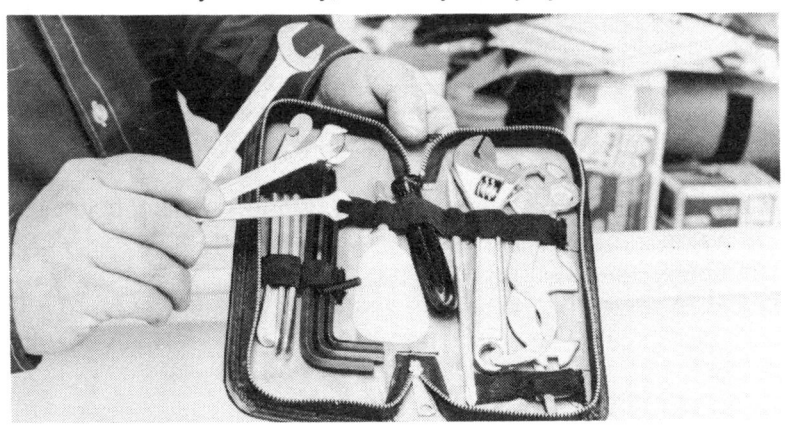

Regular cleaning not only enhances your bike's beauty, it benefits mechanical parts. One of the best habits you can develop is wiping down your bike after you ride it. Go over the frame with a damp cloth. Wipe off movable parts like the derailleur, brakes, and crank. Then go over the frame again with a soft, dry cloth. This care inhibits dirt buildup. When sludge accumulates in certain parts, it brings on wear and malfunctioning. Wiping your bike dry after a ride in the rain discourages rust. Don't hose down a multispeed bike. The water's force is too much for some parts.

Wax your bike. Some owners use a furniture polish, because auto waxes rub the finish off some bicycle paint jobs. Ask your bike dealer what he recommends for waxing your brand of bicycle. Always wash and wax your bike before you store it. Go over it again when you bring it out for the summer. If you ever sell your bike, the washing and waxing you put into it now will pay off through increased value.

Underinflated tires wear out rapidly. They turn pedaling into heavy labor. It takes only a few minutes to check pressure and pump up before you start a ride, but many cyclists neglect it.

To check multispeed tire pressures, you need a special gauge. Those for automobiles don't go high enough. Most bike tires carry 75 lb or more.

Remove the valve cap. Press the gauge onto the valve for a second or two, tightly so no air escapes from the tire. The stem will register pounds-per-square-inch (psi) of air pressure in the tire.

The recommended pressure for most tires is stamped on the sidewall. Your owner's manual should also specify how much. Do not put in more air than is needed. Less pressure, even 5 psi under, would be better than too much.

Don't use auto service-station air to inflate your bike tires. It comes out too fast for that, In a trice, the tire is overpressured and may blow out right there (. . . or wait for you to take a 20-mile ride). With experience, you'll decidedly prefer a hand pump. They cost only a few dollars. Some come with built-in pressure gauge, which saves disconnecting the hose to measure how much more pumping you need to do.

Almost anyone can repair a clincher tire. It's the inner tube that develops leaks. Once you realize the tire is going flat anyway, deflate it totally. A fast way is to unscrew the core from inside the valve stem. A little core wrench lets you do this. Push the valve stem through its rim hole and down into the casing. A tool which comes in your repair kit helps. Next, take the casing (the outer part of the tire) off the rim. Use a tire tool to pry between the tire and the rim. Use your hands to loosen the casing further. Now pull the tube out, starting from the valve stem.

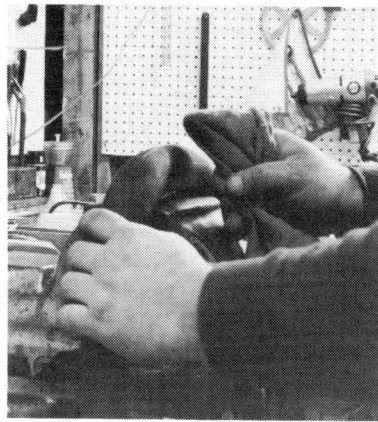 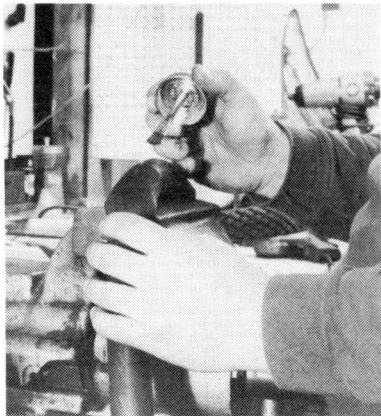

Check to see where the tube is punctured. Put air in it; then immerse it in water. Lacking water, you can inflate the tire and rotate it near your face. You may feel or hear the escaping air.

After you find the puncture, make sure the area all around the leak is dry. Use the scuffer from your tire kit to roughen the tube around the hole. Apply glue to an area around the puncture larger than the patch you're using. When the glue becomes tacky, put on the patch. Roller it down so it sticks solidly.

After the patch dries, put the tube back into the casing. If you inflate the tube slightly first, it's less likely to become twisted as you work it in. Align the valve stem with the hole in the rim. Now push the bead of the tire casing inside the rim's edge. Make sure the tire is seated around the rim evenly. Sight along the thin line that's molded along the sidewall of the tire. It should be spaced evenly all the way around. Inflate the tire and recheck the fit.

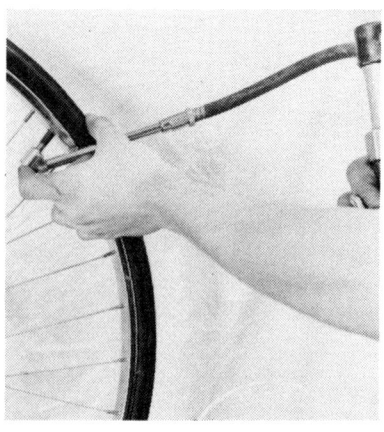

Wheel alignment depends on the tension of all the spokes. Their precise adjustments keep the rim circular, through an evenly distributed pull they exert on the rim. When one spoke pulls to much or too little, it guides the rim slightly leftward or rightward at that point. If the rim warps far enough, the tire rubs against the frame.

You correct this fault by adjusting spokes with a spoke wrench—tightening or loosening, whichever straightens the wheel. Spokes criss-cross each other as they progress around the wheel. Also, each spoke attaches to the rim opposite the side on which it attaches to the hub. This makes alignment rather complicated. Trial and error simply won't work. Adjust the wrong spokes and you could wind up with some broken ones when you test-ride the bike.

Really, this is a job best left to a bike shop. You'll have fewer headaches and regrets. It takes even a good bike technician a while to develop a feel for wheel adjustment.

You can do your part by checking alignment at least once a month. First pluck the spokes. Each should have a little "give" or resilience. Loose spokes are easy to bow and move. This leads to poor alignment. Next have someone lift the front of the bike, or gently turn it upside down on the grass (concrete scrapes it). Brace your hand against the fender, fork, or front tube, with your thumb near but not touching the wheel. Spin the wheel. If it wobbles even faintly, it will weave closer to your thumb at some points. A technician would mark these warped locations and adjust the appropriate spokes. The precisely adjusted wheel rolls smoothly without the slightest weaving when you spin it.

The *fork* is the frame member the bike's front wheel fits into. It requires little care, but it can get bent. Bumping into a wall or building usually is what does it. In bike accidents, the fork seems more susceptible to damage than most other frame parts.

Riding your bike with the fork warped can wear tires down in a hurry. The bike may seem hard to control. A really bad fork can force enough pressure and imbalance to eventually bend the frame too. Both can be straightened, but the frame will thereafter be weak. The general appearance of your bike changes since frame work usually can be spotted. You might want to consider getting rid of the bike instead of having it repaired. If you notice it early enough, you can just replace the fork.

Keeping the fork safe and true depends mainly on watching where you're headed. Don't pound across railroad tracks or jump curbs. And lay your bike down carefully if you don't use a stand.

The fit of the fork in the bicycle-frame head tube affects how well the bicycle steers. A cone and bearings inside the head tube hold the fork, and a crown nut at the top of the tube binds the whole assembly together snugly. If that crown nut gets loose, so does steering. Or, if the nut is too tight, steering is not responsive. (Other factors contribute to steering problems —particularly loose wheels or handlebars.)

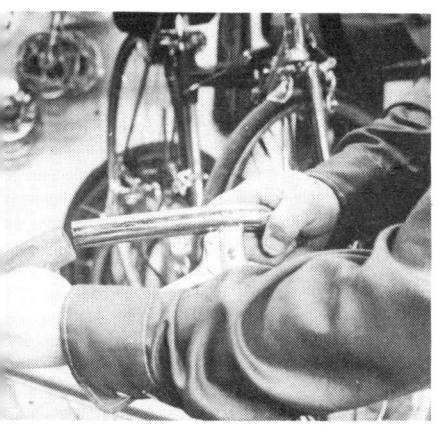 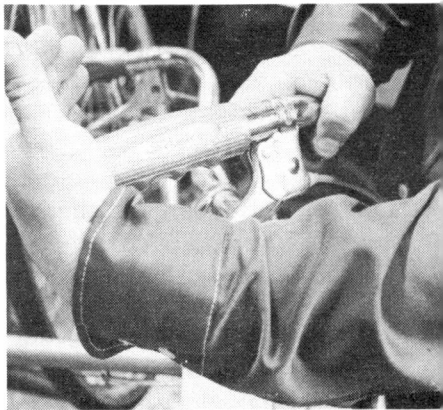

Handlebars don't need the close attention some parts do. But faults in them can be dangerous. A clamp and nut at the front of the stem allows you to adjust the drop of the handlebars —how low or high or at what angle the grips are located. If that clamp becomes the slightest bit loose, the handlebars could slip suddenly under your weight of leaning on them, particularly after you've gone over a bump or hit a chuckhole. This could cause a bad fall. Check the clamp occasionally or have your technician do it. At the same time, he can check tightness of the binder bolt and wedge (which controls the adjustment for handlebar height).

Handlebars are constructed of chrome or an alloy. Chrome can rust; alloy bars won't. Chrome cleaner keeps chrome handlebars shiny and protected. Wipe both types dry if they get wet. Don't leave your bike outside in the weather. Put a plastic cover over it or park it indoors.

Grips do more than just keep your hands from slipping off the handlebars. They protect the ends of the bars. The ends are sharp too, and in an accident could cut you. Upright handlebars take plastic or rubber grips.

Grips wear out frequently. You can make them last longer by keeping them out of sun or rain. When they begin to crack and wear, replace them. Take the old grips off. Scrape away any rubber that remains. Apply a bit of cement to the bar end. Slide the new grips on with a twisting motion, making sure the finger grooves end up on the underneath side. Then tap the end with the heel of your palm to be sure the grip is on tight.

Drop handlebars should be taped. If you don't tape them, at lease put plugs in the ends so the sharp edges don't snag you.

If you bought your multispeed bike new, the handlebars were probably taped already. The tape ages, cracks, and begins peeling off. It's easily torn by a rough cement wall, by any sharp object, or by rubbing the ground in a fall.

You can tape handlebars yourself. The photos on the opposite page detail the wrapping technique and the procedure. Begin 2 inches from the head post or stem, and work toward one end. You tape half the handlebar at a time. Wind the tape tightly around the bar several times right where you start. The tape can't be loose, or it will buckle and move later. You may want to use sticky adhesive tape to hold the end in place at first. To make the job look neater, tuck the starting end of the tape under itself on the underside of the handlebar. An exposed end may get tugged loose and mess up your whole new tape. Take the extra minute to tuck it away snugly out of sight.

Start overlapping the tape as you wind it toward the end of the handlebars. A ¼-inch overlap is sufficient. Measure if you need to; ¼ inch is less than some folks realize. Take your time and wind the tape neatly.

When you reach the end, cut the tape with enough left to push into the end of the handlebar. A button plug then holds the tape end in place. Don't hesitate to redo the job if you don't have it tight or neat enough. You don't want the taping to work loose when you're out on a long ride or in a tricky maneuvering situation. When the one side satisfies you, tape the other.

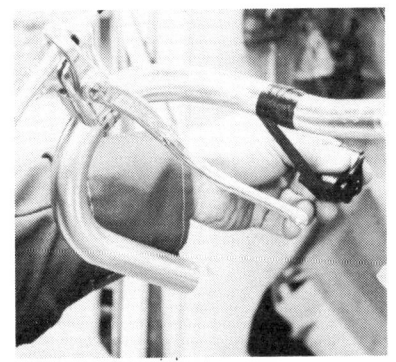
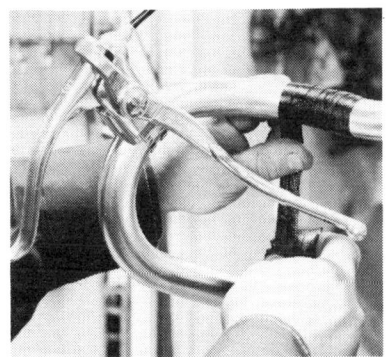
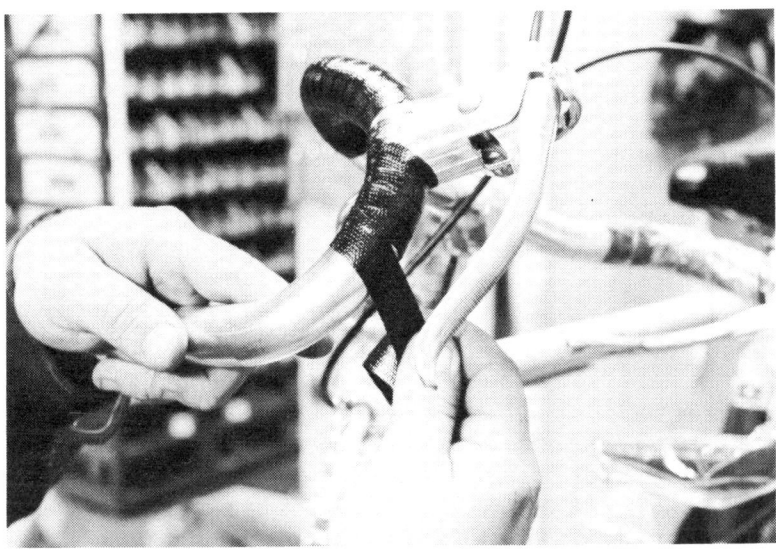

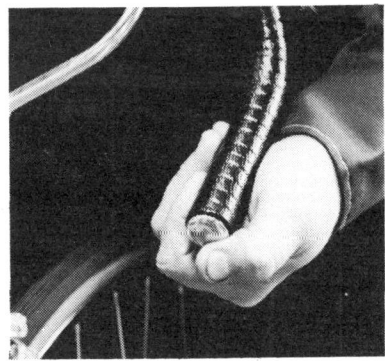

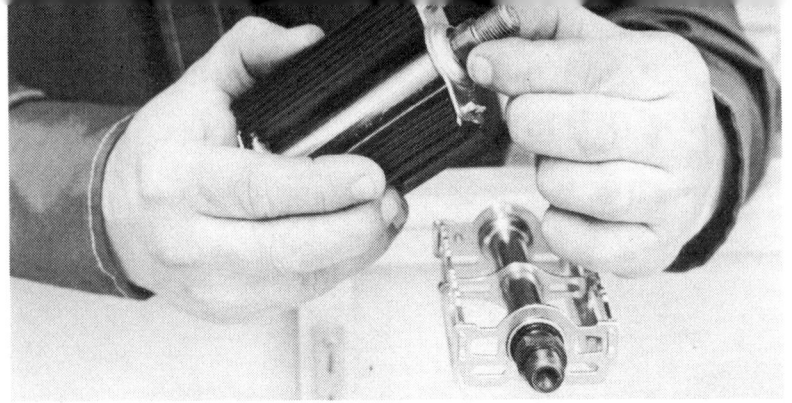

Your bike comes with either rubber or steel (rat-trap) pedals. Rubber pedals usually are standard on one-speed, three-speed, and five-speed bikes. Rubber pedals can get slippery when they're wet, which hampers safety. A rubber pad may need replacing occasionally; they do chip off or break. Constant exposure to sun and water eventually causes some rubber pedals to crack or rot.

Rat-trap pedals are constructed of steel, and are naturally more durable. Serrated edges grip your shoe sole and keep your foot from slipping off so easily. Rat-traps help you pedal more smoothly.

You can buy rat-trap pedals and add them to any bike. If you want to add toe-clips (which fit only rat-trap pedals), make sure the pedal you buy has holes for the toe-clips to attach by.

Pedals require little care. Wipe off mud and dampness after riding. Dry them if you happen to leave your bike out in the dew. The pedal has ball bearings on which it spins. Keep them free of dampness and dirt. A drop or two of fine oil once a week keeps them rolling loosely. Shaky or sticky bearings calls for a new pedal.

When the pedal goes bad, replace it immediately. Don't make riding difficult by leaving a pedal broken; you'll waste a lot of pedaling energy. And if your foot slips wrong, you may not be riding at all for a while.

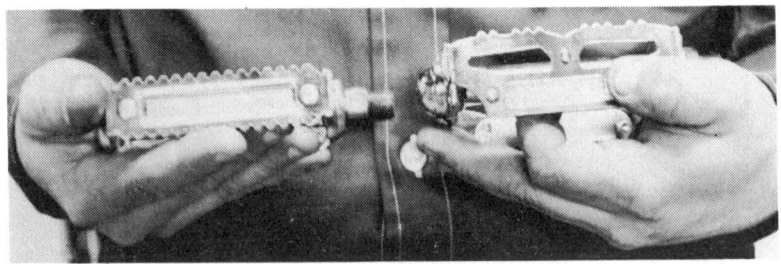

The crank converts your up-and-down foot motion to rotary energy, ultimately turning the rear wheel of the bicycle. On earlier bikes, pedals were directly a part of the front wheel. Today's pedals turn a sprocket wheel, attached to the crank, which rolls the chain that drives the rear cogs that turn the wheel.

The crank itself is simple. American cranksets consist of several separate pieces. European cranksets have the sprockets made as part of the crank rather than attached to it. European cranksets are for serious cyclists who know how to treat a bike, because construction is more delicate.

You can buy special cranks. Some are cast from alloys that make them extremely light. Specialist bike shops carry cranks priced to $90 or more.

All cranks can be broken. Young children treat bikes roughly. Dropping a bike instead of leaning it against something can bust a crank. Broken cranks can't be repaired.

Occasional attention preserves even this simple part of your bicycle. The crank should move freely as you pedal. If it seems to pull back, the chain may be too tight. Rust in the crankset bearings can cause a draggy feeling. Wiping down, as already described, and periodic lubrication can prohibit rust.

Check the crank every so often to see if there is any sideplay. Grasp the pedal, pull outward on it, and shake it. The crank shouldn't move or rattle. If it seems loose, the adjusting cone probably needs attention. Forget doing it yourself. It's easy to get too tight. Let a technician handle the adjustment. While he's at it, ask him to repack the bearing inside with wheelbearing grease.

The roller chain, called variously *bush-roller* or *sprocket-chain*, converts your energy and pressure into motion. If it becomes dirty, rusty, loose, or worn, it is no longer efficient. Easy, but regular, maintenance can head off trouble.

Dirt is your chain's worst enemy. It grinds roller links drastically. Dust mixes with oil to form greasy sludge. Wipe off excess water and dirt from the chain after a ride. Oil the chain again if needs it. After riding in snow and slush which often has salt in it, your bike needs to be washed down rather than wiped off. Remember not to use a pressure hose; you could damage the derailleur. For quick reoiling, spray-can lubricants are handy.

The chain needs lubricant at least twice a year. But you can get a chain too oily, too. A properly lubricated chain doesn't *look* oily. A light film is all that's necessary. Your finger shouldn't come away greasy and dirty from touching the chain. Excess oil and grease gather dirt.

Take a soft cloth and try to wipe off excess oil. That may be all you need to do. If the chain still looks and feels excessively oily, remove it and put it to soak overnight in kerosene or mineral spirits. Don't use gasoline; it's very unsafe. When you take the chain out of the mineral spirits, wipe it dry.

Now it needs oil. Just a light film is plenty. A silicone lubricant is less greasy than most, lubricates better, and doesn't attract as much dirt. You can use the same type to lubricate other parts of the bike.

When a chain gets rusty, soaking in mineral spirits might save it. The rust can then sometimes be wiped off. Don't keep a rusty chain.

Chain tension constitutes a common problem. A lot of riders leave the chain too tight or too loose. A tight chain can damage cogs, distort the derailleur, or break the front gear-changer. The chain could snap when you shift gears. A loose chain doesn't use your pedal power efficiently.

You can check the chain tension best by looking and feeling. A loose chain drags and bows at the bottom. Tap the bottom stretch of chain. If it's too tight, it doesn't spring back and forth.

Adjusting the chain is easiest when your bike has a quick-release rear wheel. You take up the slack by moving the rear wheel backwards. Flip the quick-release handles and pull the wheel back until the chain looks and feels right. Tighten the handles and check the chain. You might have to remove a link or have it done. If the chain is too tight, move the wheel forward until the chain has some spring to it when tapped.

With no quick-release handles, you'll need a wrench. Loosen the outside nuts slightly on each side of the wheel. If the chain is loose, pull the wheel back; if tight, move it forward. Before you tighten the nuts, carefully keep the wheel in line so it can't rub or come near the top or bottom frame members. Tighten the right side slightly, then the left. Go back and firmly tighten both.

A ten-speed bicycle has two derailing devices. One, at the rear cogs, always goes by the name *derailleur*. The front one, at the double sprocket, gets called derailleur by some, but usually is tagged *gear changer*. It's much simpler than the five-gear derailleur at the rear.

The rear derailleur throws the chain onto the appropriate cog size to give you the gear you want. Each position of the gearshift lever up front always engages a certain cogwheel.

A roller system is part of the rear derailleur mechanism. Below the actual derailing setup you'll see two small idler cogwheels. The chain follows them. These rollers serve two purposes: they guide the chain to the right cogwheel and they take up slack in the chain. Without this roller arm, the multiple-diameter (geared) drive system wouldn't work.

Derailleur repairs and adjustments are best left up to your bicycle technician. They are touchy and can be messed up without much effort. Take thoughtful care of the derailleur assembly. You'll eventually be able to recognize what repairs it needs.

Dirt, perhaps more than anything else, hurts a derailleur. It's close to the ground, so it picks up dirt easily. Lots of riding on dusty roads compounds the problem. Wiping the derailleur off gently after riding saves some wear and tear. On a bike that hasn't been kept in good condition, you can even hear the gritty sound as dirt interferes with the derailleur. It can get bad enough to impede operation, making shifts erratic.

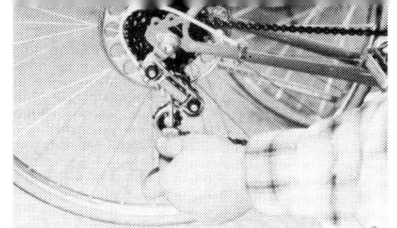 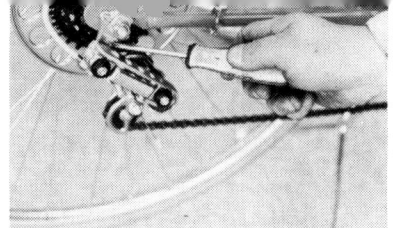

Rough treatment damages a derailleur. Don't ever drop your bike on the ground. Take a few seconds to lean it against something, and be sure it leans *away* from the derailleur side. It's the most delicate part of your bicycle, so treat it as such.

Methods of riding affect the derailleur, too. Never backpedal a multispeed bike. It's also a good idea never to roll your bike backward, but rather to pick it up and turn it around if you must change direction—even a few feet. Shift only while pedaling and shift no more than two gears at a time (see pages 62–65).

Each derailleur has a high- and low-gear limit adjustment. You should not mess with these adjustments unless the chain has a tendency to "miss" the cogwheel. These adjustment screws align the chain with the right cogwheel. If they're adjusted wrong, the chain can fall between cogs or on the axle. If it misses low gear, the chain could hit the spokes and damage them. This might also damage the wheel, the chain, the cog, and/or the rider.

Consult your owner's manual to learn where the screws are for each limit adjustment. The locations vary from model to model. Make the high-gear adjustment first. That guides the chain onto the smallest gear, the one farthest from the spokes. You'll have to shift several times after each tiny adjustment of the screw, to see if the chain drops onto the smallest cog as it should. If the adjustment won't correct the problem, shift-cable adjustment may be the answer. Take the bicycle to your technician.

Once you get high gear right, check low gear. That puts the chain onto the largest cog, next to the spokes. It has its own screw you adjust. If adjusting won't do the job, the derailleur probably has been damaged and needs expert attention.

There's one more adjustment on some derailleurs. It may not be a screw, but a wire spring you can hook at different places. It controls idler-roller tension on the chain. Set the spring so there's no hanging slack in the chain in either low or high gear.

The front derailleur or speed-changer can have the same problems the rear derailleur has. But there are only two gear wheels (sprockets) to deal with. The chain slips off either of these sprockets when the changer is poorly adjusted. You could be injured. You push down, expecting resistance. The chain slips off, and your downward force could dump you. Sitting on the seat to pedal decreases this likelihood.

The chain runs through an elongated cage just over the double-sprocket crank. The adjustment aligns the cage so it guides the chain accurately from one sprocket to the other—and back. There's often two adjustments—one coarse, and one fine. Make the coarse adjustment with the chain on the inside sprocket, and the fine adjustment on the outside one. If neither adjustment aligns the chain to shift properly, the cable may need adjusting. Don't mess too much with this assembly. The front derailleur is not as delicate or complicated as the rear one, but it does demand expert attention for certain problems.

 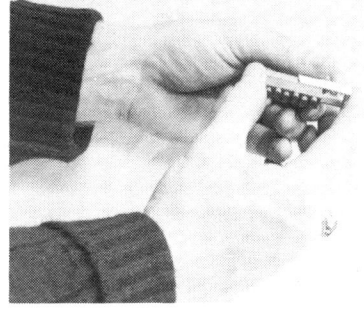

Handbrakes on multispeed bikes are more complicated than coaster brakes. Handbrakes are operated by squeezing levers on the handlebars. The left lever controls front brakes and the right lever controls the rear. Most brake service should be left to the bike technician. But, as with derailleurs, there are things you can detect and have repaired when necessary.

How you use the brakes determines their life. You have two brakes; use them both (see page 42). Using only the rear brake puts too much strain on it, causing excessive and uneven wear. This also strains the cable. An abused cable may snap sometime when you need it most.

The cables are composed of strands of fine wire. These wires can fray. Inspect them regularly, and have any frayed ones replaced. You can help avoid frayed cables. Check the way each one follows your bike to the brake. Straighten any twisting or looping. Don't play around with the cable; any wire weakens if it is bent back and forth.

You can change brake shoes. They're the parts that rub against the wheel rim. They crystallize quickly in certain climates. Replace them anyway before the grooves are worn smooth. You don't need tools. Just push out the worn shoe, and slide in the new.

When one shoe needs replacing, replace all four. They're cheap. When brakes squeak, the shoe isn't hitting the rim in a pigeon-toed position. Don't try to fix this; you could snap the metal arm. Take it to an expert.

For the brakes to work effectively, no part of the shoe should touch anything other than rim. An acorn nut in the arm lets you slide the brake to the right position. Retighten the bolt. Check front brakes and rear.

The brakes might need professional attention. When you shake the arm of the brake, it should not be loose. Neither brake should seem to stick when it's applied. It must always spring back when you release the brake lever.

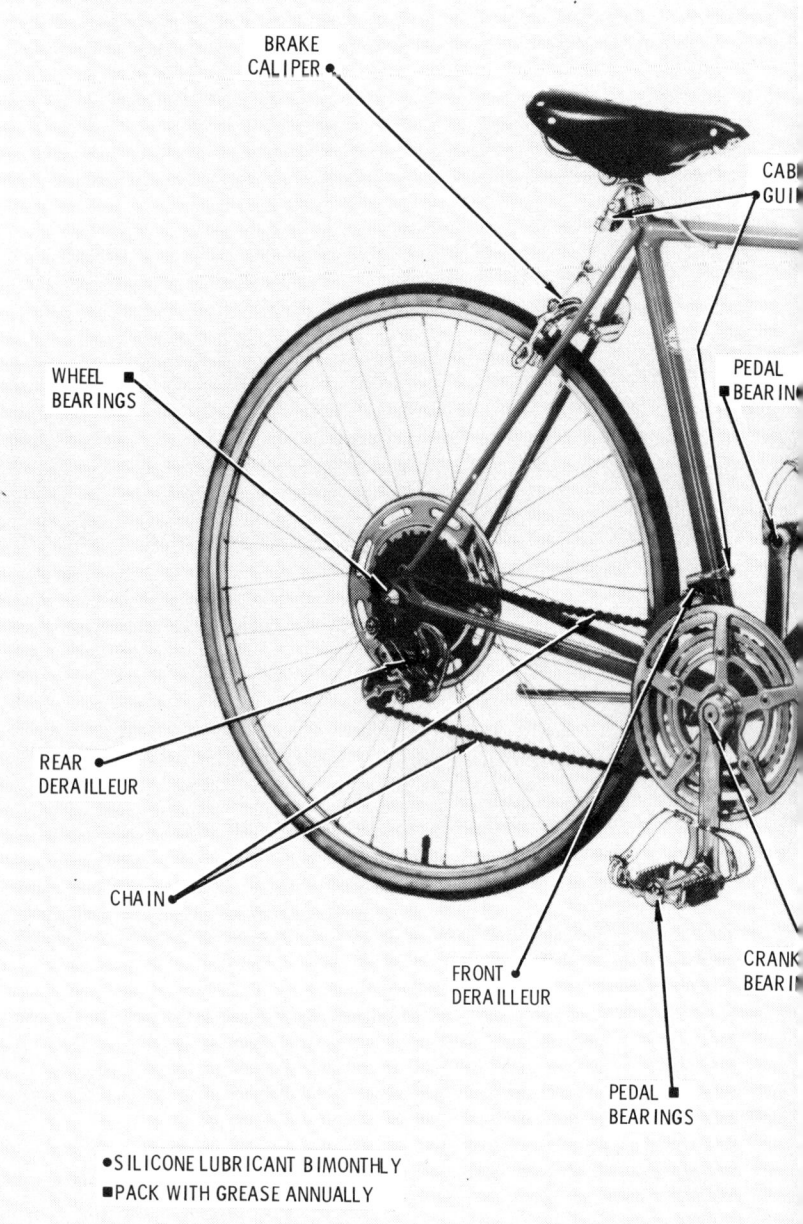

- SILICONE LUBRICANT BIMONTHLY
- PACK WITH GREASE ANNUALLY

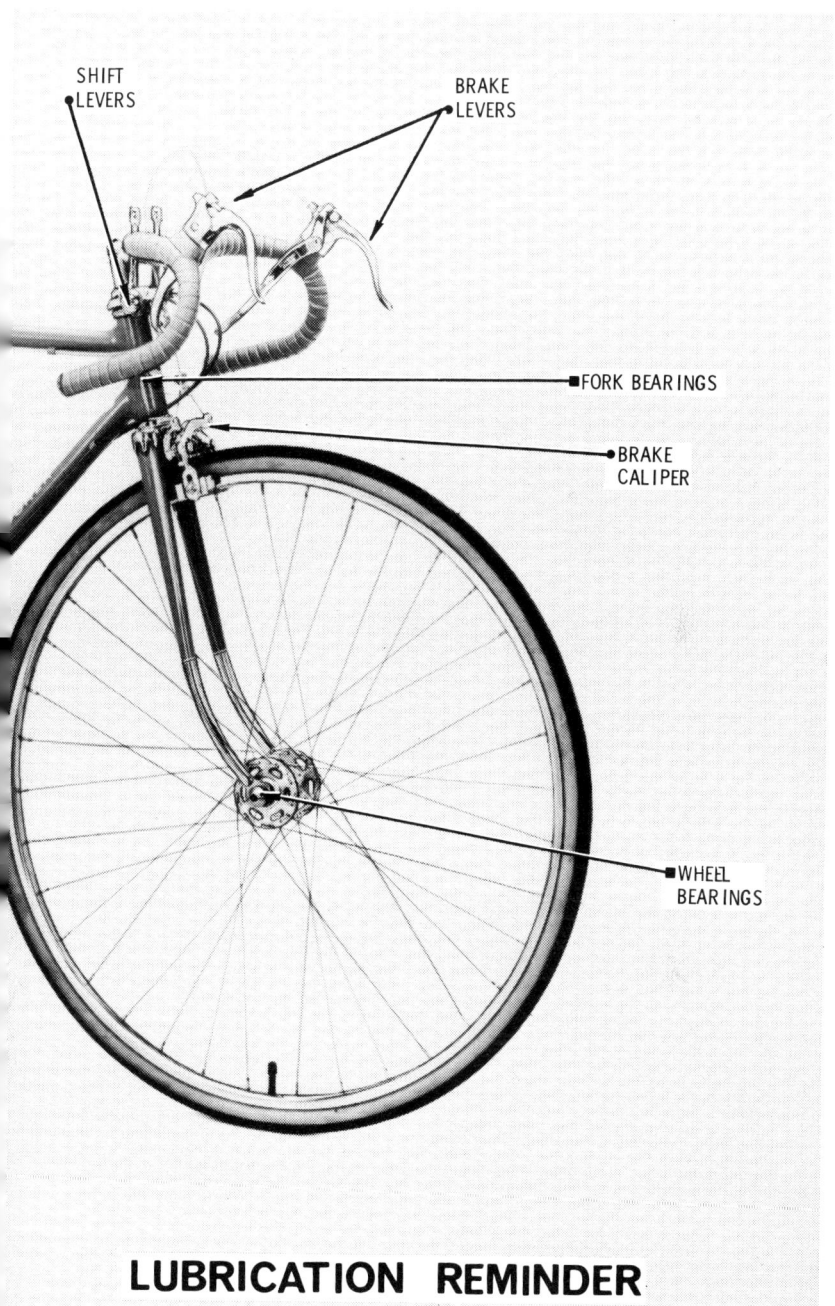

Lubrication keeps your bike in good condition, and prolongs its life. If you do much riding, you'll want to use the silicone lubricant every couple of months. Bearings should be packed once a year, preferably when you store the machine.

Do a complete lubrication job. A chart (preceding page) helps you remember all the points. Start at the back, and move forward. You may prefer to have your technician pack the bearings; it requires some disassembly.

Storing depends on how much you use your bike. If you put it away for the winter, deflate sew-up tires. Hang the bike, preferably by its rims, on hooks. Special hooks, available at most bicycle shops, screw into garage beams or walls. Never store any bike with tires on the ground, unless you plan to buy new tires next season.

Chapter 10

Clubs and Getting Together

It's typical of most people that when they enjoy something, they want to share it. Bicycling stimulates that kind of enthusiasm. Families, friends, neighbors, relatives—the more the merrier.

And that's how bicycling clubs begin. A small group of cyclists decide they can accomplish more and have a wider variety of fun as a larger group. They set out to recruit others who are drawn to cycling. Very often, a club or association springs up naturally, around some specific bicycling activity. A certain Midwest area boasts three clubs. One consists mostly of bicycle racers. Another (very large) concentrates on family touring. A third comprises college students. You could form a club of bicycle campers, for example.

Even though you may not ordinarily be a "joiner," you might extract some worthwhile benefit from a membership in a local, state, or national bicycling club. The final pages of this book illustrate some typical club functions.

Bike clubs can be serious or leisurely . . . or both. So much depends on what the membership wants. Racing clubs and touring clubs exist for their particular aspect of bicycling, and the members are serious about their activities. The only purpose of a small bike club might be recreation.

A larger membership generally branches out, with internal groups pursuing their interests in cycling. So why organize? With larger numbers, the bike club can accomplish more than individuals or a small group can. A club may be instrumental in drafting bicycle legislation and getting it passed, creating bike lanes on streets, laying out commuter routes within a city, or planning recreation routes and bike trails in parks. Bicyclists realize the importance of these things, but they know also that working on such projects takes the effort and time of many people. Active clubs have the numbers to get things done.

Many large bike clubs get involved in community activities. One works with the March of Dimes, helping raise money by sponsoring a special bike ride. Legislative lobbying includes pushing for new bike routes, to get more funds appropriated for area cycling, for better bike safety laws—and in general trying to see bicycling acknowledged as a valuable form of recreation. One example: the Central Indiana Bicycling Association (CIBA) is working out a plan that may convert miles of abandoned railroad rights-of-way into bike paths.

At meetings and afterwards, committees form to work on various activities. Involvement depends on your interests and ability. If the club has a newsletter, someone has to write it and distribute it. Routing committees spread out the countless aspects of putting a tour together, so no one has to do all the work. A special tour or event may have its own committee. A member with artistic talent may design trophies, patches, and posters, do artwork for the newsletter, or make sketches to help lobby for bike legislation.

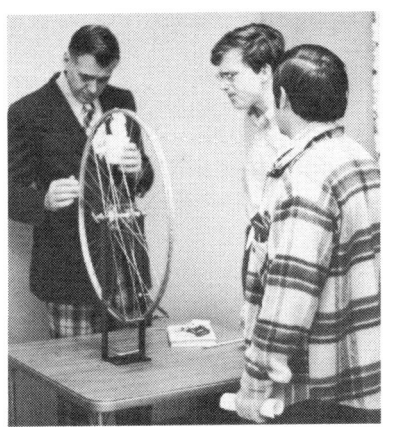 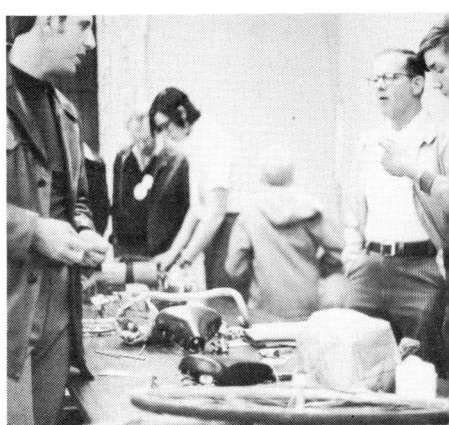

One major benefit clubs offer, at least those that aren't new, is education. You can learn a lot about cycling from experienced members. A club's teaching program might involve lectures, demonstrations, and films about many aspects of bicycling. Experts can explain and show how to take care of a bike or repair and adjust some part of it.

Many clubs offer their members workshop seminars at special events. An annual bike-club meeting, for instance, might include race-riding demonstrations, camping, workshops, lectures on safety or bike laws, and other ideas of interest to bicyclists. The club's program committee could arrange a special demonstration for each monthly meeting. Skilled members can demonstrate their specialty. Local dealers sometimes participate in or sponsor these educational workshops and demonstrations.

The social hour after a club meeting can be a time for interaction among cyclists. The "bike swap" is a creative idea. Members set up items they have to trade or for sale. Bargains pass among members. You meet cyclists who may become good friends. You learn more about cycling all the way around, at meetings of a really active club.

Plenty of clubs stir excitement and sustain membership interest through contests. Almost any kind of bicycle riding can generate some kind of competition. Oldest rider on a tour, youngest rider, fanciest custom bike, best-dressed rider, smallest bike, earliest arrival, fastest sprinter between two telephone poles, last to drop out of an endurance ride, most meetings attended, attended every meeting for a year, served on the most committees, most original idea for a bicycling event, newest bicycle on a ride, oldest bicycle, prettiest paint job, smoothest rider, and so on . . . only your imagination limits what you can set up as a contest.

One coveted and practical award can be for safety. Contestants qualify first through an oral or written exam on safety rules. Then, a series of riding contests during regular tours or on one particular weekend establish the "safe" riders. Your club could sponsor a continuing safety program with a small cloth stripe or star awarded for each year of riding without an accident of any kind at club events. You can work out details that suit your club, its membership, and the kind of riding that dominates.

A contest committee can develop competitions and oversee them. You'll find that regular contests for all ages quickly grow into the most popular activities of the club.

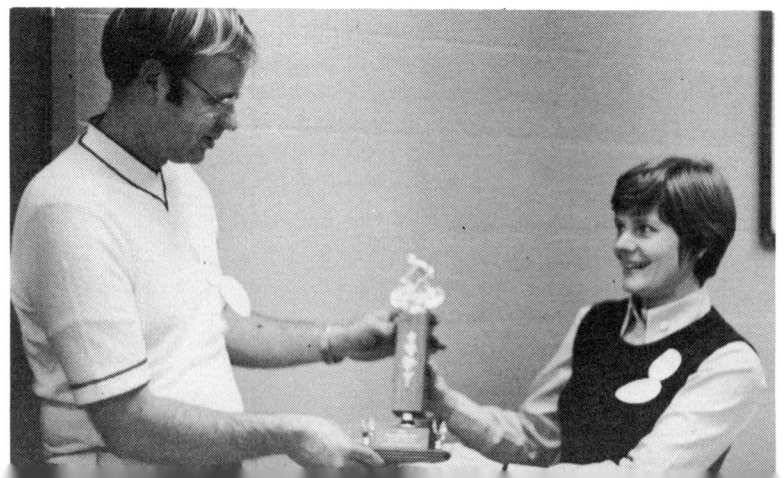

You promote bike safety best through the practical example of riding safely. Each group hike has a leader who goes over the rules of the road briefly for newcomers and as a reminder to the steadies. Encourage members to practice safety all the time. Riding with a group helps a new rider learn how to handle awkward situations. Clubs have committees to work on disseminating safety information to members.

Club committees work with 4-H Clubs, Boy Scouts, Girl Scouts, and other young people's groups. Some bike clubs conduct safety classes at community schools. At a bicycle outing, demonstrations teach safety. A new rider may go through a program on one or several Saturdays to earn a safety certificate. Clubs often work with the police department, department of transportation, or a local school to set up safety testing lanes at school or in a shopping center. The bicyclists whose machines and riding pass the inspection get safety emblems or "licenses" to display on their bikes. In this way the club helps cyclists who aren't members and shows its concern toward safe bicycling.

Such activities also draw in new members.

Organizing hikes and tours constitutes the main activity of most clubs. A lot goes on behind the scenes. Some clubs have committees to work out routing, a few give the president that responsibility, and others rotate the task. Good routing takes time.

Clubs try to tailor their overall program so everyone finds an activity which suits them. Committees set up family outings, camping trips, long-distance tours, short hikes, whatever. Limited hikes specify experience or ability, so beginner cyclists don't get discouraged. All members receive information on all rides, where to meet, what to bring, and who the leader is. They pick which hikes they feel comfortable riding in.

"Sag wagons" pick up stragglers and help cyclists with problems. The sag wagon usually carries extra tires, tubes, chains, and tools. If the club rides in winter, the sag wagon carries hot food and beverages.

Tour or hike groups need leaders. After a hike is routed, the leader drives it to check road conditions. Maps don't give the specific data the cyclist needs. Special details are noted on the map copy given each participating rider. The route must pass stores where food can be bought, unless each rider or a sag wagon carries food. Rest stops must be included, even on short hikes.

A club can earn money for itself sponsoring special events and rides. Century hikes cover 100 miles; double-centuries encompass 200 miles; a half-century hike is only 50 miles. The magazine of the League of American Wheelmen publicizes such activities by its member clubs. This way, riders can participate in the activities of other clubs. Both club and rider benefit.

Hikes with large groups, and where riders come from other areas, involve extra work. Registration becomes a necessary part of planning. Longer hikes require making motel reservations, letting riders know where they can make their own reservations, or finding camp facilities.

Most clubs sponsor these tours for income, and so charge a small fee (usually under $5). They may award certificates or patches to everyone completing a special hike. Example: The Central Indiana Bicycling Association sponsors the Hilly Hundred every autumn; the route takes cyclists through scenic Brown County, Indiana. This hike is open to riders from everywhere. As many as 700 cyclists pedal the Hilly Hundred. The CIBA hands out awards at a banquet afterward. Awards go to the youngest rider, the oldest rider, and the rider who rode the farthest on his bike to get to the event. There are other awards.

Bicycling is not an activity that needs to be "sold" to its participants. Either you're interested or you're not. The pages of this book set forth most of what you need to know if you're considering becoming a bicyclist. Your next step is to select the bicycle that suits the kind of riding you want to do, learn to ride it safely and smoothly, and then maintain it carefully.

Whether you ride with a club, go it alone, or just pedal around the countryside with friends; whether you ride in races, take 100-mile touring hikes, or cycle coast-to-coast; whether you discover your own neighborhood on a three-speed or explore new mountain vistas on a precision ten-speed . . . you'll find any place you ride a bicycle brings you the feeling and thrill of

THE OPEN ROAD